Texts:
Maria Pia Girolami
Michael Lee

Photos:
Dino Ganzaroli

Verona

Edizioni KINA Italia / L.E.G.O.

2

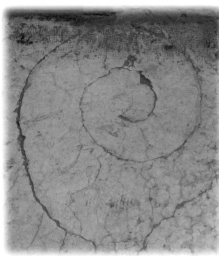

HISTORICAL INTRODUCTION

Not only in its museums, but even simply strolling through Verona's streets one sees, a little everywhere, testimonies of distant epochs, some so remote that they date to a time before the existence of the earth on which Verona today stands.

60 million years ago the entire area was under sea level. In the red marble of the streets and of the houses one finds, still today, fossilised sea-creatures. Some 400,000 years ago, people began to frequent the hills of the area. These are riddled with caves, some still bearing fragments of paintings. Chosen, above all, because they were rich in the flint from which spears and axes were made, these became an obligatory stop in the seasonal migrations of hundreds of thousands of years.

After the end of the last ice-age, people began to raise beasts and cultivate the lands where Verona would rise. The beginnings of Verona can be sought in fact on the hill of San Pietro rising behind the present-day city directly above the river. The name Verona itself may indicate this position: Ona, present in the name of hill towns, perhaps means hill; Ver may stem in some way from waters.

The small village here proved to be in a highly strategic position. The construction of roads made it important in the consolidation of Roman influence. The Via Postumia linked Genoa with

On pages 2, 3: an aerial view of the Arena and 12th century walls.

Above: a fossil in Verona marbles; Right: an aerial view of the city and the Arena.

4

Aquileia on the Venetian lagoon, the Via Gallica with France, and the Via Claudio-Augusta with Austria, and these three roads crossed here. Verona became a Roman Municipality in 49 BC, its citizens becoming, at this point, Roman citizens. Rebuilt on the typical Roman military grid plan, down in the curve of the Adige river, it had two main roads meeting in the central Forum (Piazza Erbe): the Cardus Maximus (Via Leone) north-south, the Decumanus Maximus (Via Porta Borsari) east-west, and a series of streets parallel to these meeting at right-angles forming blocks. These form the street plan of the centre still today. The city was surrounded by a ring of walls, parts of which still stand. In these walls opened the two main gates which we see today: Porta Leona (The Lions Gate), and Porta Borsari (The Bursars' Gate). Rebuilt in stone, the Bridge of San Pietro marked

the entrance of the Via Postumia into town. Testimony to Verona's importance is its theatre: one of the first, and most magnificent, to have been built in stone. In the 1st century A.D. the Amphitheatre "Arena", was built, too. Today it hosts one of the most famous Opera festivals in Europe. Moreover, shortly after its absorption into Roman culture, Verona provided one of the greatest poets of Latin literature: Catullus, fervent defender of Roman liberty, in the moment when Julius Caesar was dismantling the Republic.
When the seat of western Roman administration moved, from Rome, north to Milan and then Ravenna, Verona became likewise important for the running and defence of the territories, retaining this position during the succession of occupations by northern, non-Italian peoples (the "Barbarians"): here the main battle among

Odoacre e Theodoric took place, Theodoric chose it as his residence (he is still known as Theodoric of Verona), here the Longobard kings came to live and the story of Rosmund took place, together with the stories of Bertoldo.
The Romans had used Romanised Germanic populations to police their frontiers and act as mercenaries. A wage revolt in the ranks contributed to the fall of the Western Roman Empire in 475, bringing Odoacre and his mercenaries, the Eruli, in power in Italy, but when they began to threaten the territories of the Eastern (Byzantine) Empire, the Emperor asked another Germanic population, the Ostro-Goths under Theodoric, to intervene. Ousted from Verona (489), Odoacre eventually took refuge in Ravenna. After a three year siege Theodoric invited Odoacre to a banquet and murdered him.

However, on the entrance of the church of San Zeno this betrayal is transformed into a knightly joust. Thoroughly Romanised, having spent his childhood a hostage in Constantinople, Theodoric retained the apparatus of Roman administration, promulgating a code of laws which regulated the co-existence of Gothic and Roman populations. Verona became one of his preferred residences. History remembers him as Theodoric of Verona. He and his court resided on the hills of San Pietro. Towards the end of his life, in a climate of renewed hostility with the Byzantine Empire, Theodoric, an Arian Christian like his people, began to doubt the loyalty of his Catholic Roman councillors. He had a number, including Boetius (The Consolation of Philosophy) executed, and is therefore portrayed, once again at San Zeno, as having fallen into to Hell while hunting a mysterious deer. The Byzantine Emperor Justinian began a series of wars aimed at re-establishing his direct control over the Western territories. In Italy these ultimately had the effect of destabilising the Gothic realm, paving the way for a further invasion, that of the Lombards, who, unlike their predecessors, had not undergone a process of Romanisation. With

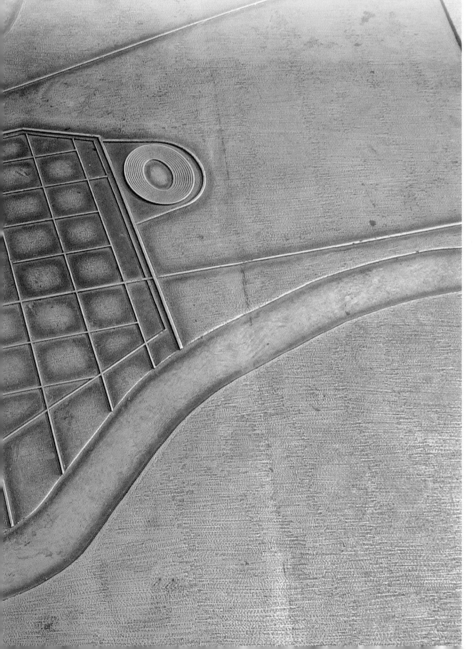

their occupation (569) Roman Verona ceases to exist.

The Lombards were Arian Christians, and on the pretext of aiding the Pope, Charlemagne, King of the Franks (later first Holy Roman Emperor) conquered Italy. Verona succumbed in 775. Charlemagne introduced, or institutionalised, many innovations, amongst them: the idea of Europe, Feudalism, the exaggeration of the cult of the relics, a clause in the Doctrine of the Trinity which eventually led to the division between Catholicism and Orthodoxy, and so on.

Here however, he left much of the Longobard nobility intact, limiting himself to the appointment of a Frankish Count, his son Pipin. Local tradition holds that Pipin is buried in the monastery of San Zeno. During the period of Feudal decentralisation and power struggle, after Charlemagne, the crown of Italy fell to Berengario I Marquise of Friuli. During a revolt in Verona, Berengario, against the sage council of his advisors, left his house (on the site of the Roman theatre) to confront the mob, paying with his life for this audacity. This was the period of the Hungarians. Verona was sacked repeatedly, and its outlying areas and churches put to the torch. Part of the unrest, under Berengario, may have been caused by his willingness to settle this people within his realm, using them as troops. In fact, graves have been found, in the territory, with horses buried alongside the humans. These may belong to Hungarians. Adelaide and the end of The Kingdom of Italy. Berengario's son Lothario, not yet of age, became King of Italy under the regency of his uncle Berengario II. Lothario was married off to the delectable Adelaide, which union ended when the uncle poisoned his nephew. Amongst the contenders for the hand of

Left: Map of the Roman city in Via Mazzini;
Above: "Tomb of Pippin" at the Church of Saint Zeno.

the young widow, legitimate Queen of Italy, was the uncle himself. Adelaide, preferring any fate to the prospect of marriage with her husband's assassin, was imprisoned in Rocca del Garda, near Verona, there to remain until she should repent of her obstinacy. She smuggled however, a letter to the Emperor of Germany Otto I. If he liberated her she promised to marry him. Needing no other incitement than the plea of a damsel in distress, Otto I descended from his northern fasts, liberated the Queen, married her, and united Italy to his dominions.

In the year 999 Verona passed under the control of the Emperor of Germany Otto I and then of his descendants. However, the German Emperors were distant, and soon the northern Italian cities developed institutions of self-government, process sporadically disturbed by the Emperors' efforts to settle the cities' interminable wars.

To this period belong the struggles between Ghelfs and Ghibellines (anti and pro Empire forces). Given its position guarding the passes to Germany, Verona tended to find itself on the Guibelline side supporting the Empire.

In the Twelfth century Verona was ruled for a period by the tyrant Ezzelino da Romano whose family, originally under the Emperor's aegis, began to form a regional state in the North-East. His sister Cunizza, despite her interesting love-life, is to be met in Dante's Heaven. Ezzelino instead, in Hell, despite his efforts to reinforce Orthodoxy famously massacring heretics near the church of St Stephen.

Deserving of mention at this point is the foundation, in Verona, of the Tribunal of the Inquisition, by Emperor Frederick Barbarossa and Pope Lucius III (1184). The Pope's tombstone can be seen in the Cathedral.

After the interlude of Ezzelino, began the rise of the Scala family, wool merchants who would briefly make Verona capital of a regional state. Their family graves are one of the monuments most characteristic of Verona.

Following the murder of his brother Mastino "Captain of The People" (a species of police captain/mayor), Alberto was conceded temporary emergency powers in 1277. Other members of the family succeeded him, still with these powers. The title enabled them to dispose of public money. Cangrande then became official representative of the Holy Roman Emperor able to administer justice. Finally, Mastino II was invested with powers as representative of the Pope. Hence, every class surrendered its power into their hands.

Favouring local commerce at all costs, they reduced frontier duties by pursuing a policy of

Above: Lion of St Mark, symbol of Venice;
Below: The Rocca del Garda, where Queen Adelaide was imprisoned.

conquest, eventually extending their domains to a good deal of the modern Veneto, part of Lombardy and Trentino, and part of Tuscany. Thus, they came into conflict with other emerging states. This and the tax burden of maintaining armies led to their downfall. Verona was conquered first by the Visconti of Milan and then by Venice (1405). Venice faced the same problems in its expansion towards the Italian mainland, and, in the league of Cambrai, all important powers amassed against her. At Agnadello Venice was defeated, barely surviving. Verona was occupied by Maximilian, Hapsburg Emperor, until 1517 when the city was ransomed back from the cash starved Emperor. It remained Venetian until the Napoleonic invasion.

From 1796, year of Napoleon's arrival, Verona passed four times from French to Austrian occupation: Napoleon defeated the Austrians in Lombardy. These took refuge in the Venetian territories of Peschiera and Verona, where there was also the heir to the French throne. Unable to oust them, Venice declared itself neutral. This was Napoleon's pretext for an invasion.

Initially welcomed by the middle-class, heavy taxes for the army, requisitions, and the confiscation of lands belonging to the Church, soon turned popular sentiment against him. In 1797 this broke out in revolt. The episode is known as the "Pasque Veronesi" (The Veronese Easter) and was harshly suppressed. With the Treaty of Campoformio (1797) Verona was then given to the Austrians. The Venetian Republic, after a thousand years, ceased to exist. With the Treaty of Lunèville: Lombardy and The Veneto were reappropriated by the French up to the frontier of the Adige river. Verona was thus divided in two: inside the curve of the river, French; beyond (Veronetta), Austrian.

With the Peace of Presburg the Austrians were forced out of the

Veneto, which, united to the other north Italian territories, became part of the Kingdom of Italy under Napoleon. The Veronese therefore, were subject to military levy, and marched to defeat with the French, freezing to death in the Russian winter. Concrete legacies of Napoleon remain in the numbers on every door, in the reduced number of churches and monasteries, and in the grave-yards beyond the city confines: innovations of the period. The presence of Veronese art works in the Louvre is another lasting inheritance.

Napoleon defeated, the Congress of Vienna re-established the status quo. With the exception of the Venetian Republic. Verona remained an Austrian city until its unification with Italy (1866). Under the Austrians, Verona, with Mantua, Peschiera, and Legnago became part of the "quadrilateral", the bastion defending their Italian possessions. Some 20,000 sons of Verona went to soldier in the far-flung reaches of Empire, while the city became a garrison. In the shadows, here as elsewhere, "Carbonara" secret societies and subversives fomented rebellion, espousing, now this alternative, now that, but always the ideal of Italian nationhood. For instance, Countess Serego-Alighieri hid a ring of patriots who were later dispersed or arrested. Finally, after numerous rebellions and three wars, Italy became more than a geographical expression. In 1886 Verona was united, under the Savoy Kings, to the new Italian State. Today Verona has a population of some 250,000 inhabitants and a well-balanced economy based on agriculture, industry, commerce and tourism.

Above: Bombardment damage inflicted by French in 1797
Below: Ghibelline battlements. Verona was Ghibelline in the period characterised by the power-struggle between supporters of the Holy Roman Empire (Ghibellines) and the Pope (Ghelfs).

On pages 10,11: The Arena Festival.

ARENA

The Roman Amphitheatre (from the Greek: "double theatre") owes the name "Arena" (sand) to the strata of sand spread in the centre, absorbing blood and cushioning falls.

Built at the beginning of the 1st century AD, some 50 years before the Colosseum of Rome, it was one of the first permanent examples, even though the first Roman gladiatorial games had been held in 264 BC. It remained the third largest.

Externally it measured about 153m by 124m, and was some 30m. high. The oval has 44 marble tiers, supported by 4 concentric galleries, with 72 arches which corresponded to particular entrances. It was able to contain roughly 30,000 people, more than the population of the city itself, testimony to Verona's importance as a communication centre.

Of the external decorative wall, composed of three levels of arches separated by Toscanic semi-columns, only a small segment, the so-called "Ala" (wing), remains.

This was originally surmounted by a crown of square openings, which survived into the 16th century. The aspect presented today, with its combination of brick and stone, would not originally have been visible, but may give rise to the Romanesque red and white striped motif ubiquitous in Verona. Decorated with marble, the

structure is of river stones and brick, while the volts are a mixture of stones and poured cement.

Each entrance, or vomitorius, was numbered, and although entrance was free, the bottom seats were reserved for the most important citizens. It may have had a covering of fabric which protected the spectators from rain and sun.

It hosted fights between gladiators, and between men and beasts.

Originally outside the city walls, after the first Barbarian incursions it was included, for defence purposes, inside. During the middle-ages it was used as a fortress. It witnessed trials by arms and fire, proofs which those accused of crimes were forced to undergo. It was scene of capital punishments. The arches became workshops, shops and bordellos. Some sustain that its form suggested the layout of hell to Dante Alighieri (The Divine Comedy). In contrast, festivals were here held in occasions of importance: jousts, tournaments, bull fights and weddings. Moreover, St Francis of Assisi and St Anthony of Padua preached here. For

Left and Above: some views of the arches of the Arena and its "Ala" (wing).

centuries the Arena was used as a source of construction material, this often encouraged by Government, until in 1450 an edict recognised its value, and forbade the extraction of stones and the precious lead hooks which linked them. During WWII it was utilised as an air-raid shelter.

On the 10th of August 1913 a performance of Aida was held in occasion of the hundredth anniversary of the birth of Giuseppe Verdi. Since then, every summer, with the exception of the World Wars, there has been an Opera Festival attracting people from all over the world.

For Christmas, there's an exhibition of Nativities from all over the world under the Arena arches, together with a huge Christmas Star, which, starting from the top of the Arena, arrives to the middle of the square. During the Middle Ages when Roman building techniques had been lost, the Arena so impressed that a legend sprang up: A man had been condemned to death, but could have his life

saved if he were able to build the biggest and most beautiful building ever seen in one night. Desperate, he asked for the Devil's help, who built the Arena. Even the Devil, however, couldn't complete it, it was too much even for Him. This is why the Arena hasn't got a complete external ring. It was nonetheless so impressive, that his life was spared.

The Arena in Verona is protected by the UNESCO as a World Heritage.

Above: Particular of the "Ala" (wing).
Below: Night time view of Bra' Square with the Christmas Star.

PIAZZA BRA

The area beyond the walls, where the Romans built the "Arena", is named "Bra" from the German for broad. It was long used as a dump, and remained peripheral to the city. Once inserted within the city walls (XII century) markets and festivals were held here. Still today, the market/festival of St. Lucy takes place here between December 11th and 13th. With the Scala enlargement of the city (XIV cen.) the square became central, and with the opening of a road to the new gate (Porta Nuova) it became important, so that, in the Venetian period, rich families, military establishments and important Academies built their seats here. In the 1700s the "Liston", the pavement before the Palaces, was built, and became Verona's fashionable promenade.

Goethe, in his "Italian Travels" describes encounters between the gentry who arrived in carriages, or, in winter, in sleighs. With the planting of the central garden, and the construction of Palazzo Barbieri, in the 1800s, it achieved its present form.

Gardens - With the entrance of Verona into a unified Italy (1866) there was an effort to erase the memory of the Austrian military presence.

Their parade ground was transformed into a garden. Many of the most important events in post-unification history have left their mark here.

A statue of the first Italian King, Victor Emmanuel II, still stands - despite his family subsequent banishment from Italy -, where a previous statue commemorated the Venetian dominion. A second statue commemorates the partisan struggle against Nazi-fascism. Between the two, a plaque remembers the extermination of the Italian Jews. The fountain was donated by Munich with which Verona is twinned, the two cities represented on either side of the Alps.

The Liston - The "Lista" was, in Venice, the strip around Embassies where one enjoyed political asylum, the only part of the street actually paved. When, between 1770-86,

Above: Plaque recording UNESCO's recognition of Verona as "Patrimony of Humanity", World Heritage City.
Below: The Fountain in Bra Square
On page 15, Above: The Philharmonic Theatre;
Below: Statue of Vittorio Emanuele II, first King of Italy after unification.

this area was paved, for its impressive length and breadth, it became the big "Lista" (List-on).

The wall of palaces, with their porticoes, seems to mirror the Arena.

This particular was, in reality, imposed by the need to preserve a public passage to the Gate in the walls. However, continued in various epochs, in various parts of the square, the motif is probably not entirely casual. At No.2, **Palazzo Campagna**, in neo-classical style, seat of the Literary Society since the 1800s. At No.16, **Palazzo degli Honorij** is the work of Verona's great Renaissance architect Sanmichieli.

Of the second half of the 1500s, the alternation of forms from the classical lexicon lightens, like the arches of the Arena, the sense of weight, produced by rough stone work, inherited from the tradition of central Italy. At No.18, **Palazzo Righettini.** From its balcony Garibaldi should have pronounced, to the newly Italianised Veronese, an incitement to the conquest of The Papal States.

However, having just learned that his fiancée was pregnant by another, he limited himself to a

"Rome or Death", cutting short both speech and stay in Verona.

A plaque at the balcony records this war-cry. On the façade, a "Virgin Mary with Child and Angels" by G.F. Caroto.

At No.20 **Palazzo Guglienzi**, of the 15th century, with 18th century additions, and a Madonna with Child by Francesco Morone of the beginning of the 16th. At No.26, **Palazzo Ottolino** of the end of the 18th century, is in the style of Sanmichele.

The Philharmonic Academia - Still continuing the portico motif, the Accademia Filarmonica, founded in 1543, preserves a great number of musical works both printed and handwritten and a precious and rare collection of antique musical instruments: wind and cord instruments. Together with those of the Library of the Canons' Chapter they attract eminent scholars of musicology and of the realisation of antique scores.

The Philharmonic Theatre - Built for the Academia in 1732 by the architect Bibiena, it was completely destroyed by fire in 1749. Rebuilt, a portico was added on the side facing the entrance, in order to allow the nobles to get out of their carriages without getting wet. This was then elongated up to the edge of the building in 1929 by the architect Fagiuoli. Hit by a bomb during WWII, it was promptly rebuilt.

The Maffei Museum - Built as the seat of the Academia (Curtoni, 1604). Its models are: the architecture of Palladio, not only in the architectural elements, but in the inexpensiveness of the materials used (wood, brick, plaster); and columns which used to be found around Piazza Erbe.

In 1772, Scipione Maffei, passionate antiquarian, here placed, on the walls of the courtyard, his collection of Etruscan, PaleoVeneto, Greek, Latin, and Hebrew epigraphs. One of the first archaeological museums created with scientific parameters, it is still an obligatory stop for epigraphists the world over.

Portoni della Bra - The two gates in the XII century walls were opened to lead to a new 16th century gate.

The walls maintained a second line of defence, and define a thousand years of expansion given that the Arena marks the confines of the Roman city, the gate a further eight hundred, opening as it does on Corso Porta Nuova which leads to the Scala walls within which the city was confined until the unification of Italy.

The Great Guard (Gran Guardia) continues the porticoed Arena motif. Started, at the beginning of the 1600s, to allow Venetian military exercises even on rainy days, the upper level was to house a school for noble Officials. Leaning on the walls for economic motives, it was completed only in 1853, and the steps were added in the early 19th century, when it was decided to lower gradually the level of the square towards the Arena.

Palazzo Barbieri - From Barbieri, the architect. Today it is the Town Hall. Here, in the XV century, was the infamous quarter of St.Agnese, with the eponymous church. In 1520, the Hospital of The

Above: The Great Guard Palace;
Left: Carriage ride in Bra' Square.

Misericordia was built here, perhaps to confront the diffusion of the new diseases arrived from America, considering the high percentage of prostitutes who populated the area. In the second half of the 18th century a second hospital was built in the centre of the square, known as the Misericordia Nuova (New).

Both demolished in 1819, the Palace was built as seat of the Civic Guard, which, in the revolution year of 1848, became a military headquarters. Almost destroyed during the carpet bombing of WWII, only the façade remains.

The posterior has been rebuilt as a semi-circle to recall the Arena. A 14th century Gothic column at the beginning of via Mazzini, similar to the one in Piazza Erbe, represents the Virgin Mary and Saints James, Anthony Abbot and Martin. The column probably protected the nearby market. The Saints, in fact, are respectively the protector of pilgrims, of animals, and of the

harvest and also of joyous people. Today, there are the remnants of this market in the feast of Saint Lucy, held on the 13th December. Saint Lucy is the protector of minstrels, musicians and of sight (she was martyred by having her eyes carved out). However, it may also have to

do with the even older celebration of the winter solstice. During this feast, rather than Father Christmas, a maid riding on a donkey, representing Saint Lucy, brings presents to the children.

On top: The "Liston" in Bra' Square; Above: The Barbieri Palace.

VIA MAZZINI

Traditionally Via Nuova (New Street), it was created during Milan's domination, after a revolt, to provide easy access from their garrison to the centre.

The present name commemorates a hero of Italian nationalism. Its beginning, behind the Arena, marks the limit of the Roman city. At about this point there is the <u>Farmacia Due Campane</u> (Two Bells Pharmacy), from the bell foundry here.

Loggia Arvedi - (1816, Barbieri) Note the low relief representing Hercules and the lion in the tympani. The central body, slight jutting with ashlar walls, has three arches on the bottom level and a "loggia" (open space) with ionic columns and a balustrade on the second level. It was the town house of this family of wealthy silk merchants who still have a villa in the outskirts of the city. Many of their properties were sold to finance the war against the Austrians. The Arvedi family was in the 800s one of the most active families in the movement to annex the Veneto to Italy. A number of family members died in the explosion of a steamship on Lake Garda: the boat was probably blown up by Austrian plotters.

Palazzo Confalonieri - At No.28, has a beautifully sculpted portal and a fine court with Gothic stairway and well.

The Hotel Accademia - In Via Scala, was seat of the Philharmonic Academy, part of that tradition which from the late 1500s brought like-minded people together for discussion and study, but in this case admitted only those nobles who could demonstrate that neither they, nor their parents, had ever worked. Under the balcony there is a Roman sculpture with a triton playing music.

The church of Santa Maria della Scala - built by the Scala family in the early 1300s, contains frescoes with stories of Saint Jeremy (early XV century), fine examples of late Gothic painting.

San Tomio - The church of San Tomaso Apostol (or San Tomio) was rebuilt after WWII. In front of it, paved on the road, some darker stones indicate the apse of the <u>Roman Basilica</u>, whose remains are to be found underneath.

The Jewish Ghetto - The slightly higher buildings at the end of Via Mazzini, are what remains of the Ghetto. It was founded in the 1500s when Venice, to recuperate some part of the price paid to ransom Verona from the Emperor, sold the right of settlement to a Jewish community. Before the Venetian period the Jews didn't have the right to live in the city. They could own properties only in the nearby villages, which in some cases still have names associated with those families. Their activities were mainly the lending of money at rates set by government, or the selling of used clothes. (Often they sold new clothes as used, because they were not allowed to commerce new items). Some also worked as doctors. Generally, therefore, jobs not permitted to Christians. In certain periods the Jews had to wear a yellow cap (signs of recognition are typical: prostitutes for example had a blue cap, while merchants a blue sleeve). The ghettos in Venice and Verona were conceived for the protection of the Jews. Only in the ghetto could they own properties or shops and sell the items connected with their religion. Toponyms, like the nearby Corte di Spagna, recall the settlements of many Jews at the end of the 15th century when Queen Isabella of Spain expelled them. The Jewish population, soon too numerous for the area assigned them, built upwards, and these are the first "skyscrapers" of the city. After Napoleon's opening of the Ghetto the community dispersed, the area fell into disrepair, and was destroyed after WWI. Today there remain only the houses which face Piazza Erbe. The synagogue was rebuilt, but, after the decimation of WWII, for a time the community was too small (with fewer than ten persons) to hold celebrations.

CORSO PORTA NUOVA

In the XVI century, Sanmichele, Verona's great Renaissance architect, obtained permission to demolish the obsolete Milanese fortified stronghold, and to sell off the area, raising funds for the renovation of the city defences, only partly financed by Venice. The street was to be a monumental entrance to the city. Sadly, it was devastated during WWII by bombs intended for the station. Hence, the area seems modern. However, there are points of interest.

Pentagonal defensive tower - of the 14th century Vi-scontean (Milanese) citadel, it defended a bridge over the moat around the city walls. Note the difference in the height of the streets on either side of the walls.

Santa Maria della Giara - At the end of Vicolo Ghiaia (Little Sandy Street, so named for the deposits of sand left in various floods of the moat), there was the church of Santa Maria della Giara (Saint Mary of the Sands). It was built as a thank-you gift to Mary, by the Umiliati (married

communist monks, a species of Catholic Amish). They had prostrated themselves, dressed in the white of purity and innocence, before Emperor Frederick Barbarossa (second half of the XII century), to obtain his clemency for a number of their fellows accused of non-orthodox religious practice.

INA Palace - Built in its imposing mass in 1937. During the war it was seat of the SS where many citizens were tortured.

The Church of San Luca - On the other side of the street, was a refuge for pilgrims belonging to the Knights of Malta in the XII century. The Baroque altar is worth a look.

Monument to Michele Sanmichieli - Born in Verona of a family of masons, he worked the first years of the XVI century at the service of the Medici Pope Leo X in Rome. After the sack of Rome (1527) by Imperial troops, he was part of the exodus of artists which returned to their homes importing the Roman experience to the rest of Italy.

On page 18: The Arvedi Loggia.

Above: The "Portoni della Bra"', the entrance to the Square, with the Pentagonal Tower of the Visconti Citadel.
Left: Statue of Michele Sanmichieli.

THE CITY WALLS

After the defeat of Cambrai (1509), Venice ceased its expansion, consolidating and fortifying its territories. Verona was given a new system of defence. Against the new importance of artillery, the medieval walls were lowered and made broader. Systems of moats, walls, mined galleries and bastions were constructed. Positions in the surrounds, considered strategic, were fortified. This system was reinforced again by the Austrians when they made Verona one of the strongholds of the famous "Quadrilateral", the defence of their Italian possessions. Substantial fragments are still visible.

Porta Nuova - The name means New Gate and it's called like this because there hadn't previously been an entrance at this point. Built in 1540 it gives its monumental contribution to the urban landscape. In rusticated stone-work, it consisted of the central entrance, and two lateral passages for pedestrians. The other two were added by the Austrians. With a draw bridge, it was preceded by external fortifications, removed to aid traffic.

The Monument to The Fallen of Cephalonia - When Italy surrendered to the allied troops (1943), the division of Acqui decided to fight on against the Germans.

Abandoned to their fate by the Allies and Italians, their ammunitions exhausted, they surrendered. Instead of being taken prisoners, they were massacred. More than 6000 people, mostly Veronese, died in this way.

Various bastions, usually named after

Above: Evolution of the walls;
Below: Porta Nuova (New Gate).

20

the proximity of the bastions, its vaults reinforced with earth and pebbles. Avant-guard for an epoch just beginning to confront the horrors of modern war, it could contain as many as a 1000 patients, had ramps for the stretchers, and luminous rooms facing on an internal courtyard. Its baptism by fire came during the War of Italian Unification in 1866, and it proved insufficient, by far, for the thousands of wounded, in large part Italian, cared for by Italians, in an Austrian hospital.

necessity of raising their skirts. Moreover, runners were derided, and buckets of water thrown at them. Hence, prostitutes were recluted, using the occasion to reclute, in their turn, clients. It came to be known as The Palio of The Whores. Later, a Donkey race was added. Finally, after Saint Bernard of Siena preached against its degeneracy, it was suppressed. Today it has become part of the celebrations of the 1st of May, with a procession in costume, and jousting. Palio Gate is again the work of Sanmichieli, and the most monumental of its series, with five entrances, semi-columns in rusticated

nearby monasteries, can still be seen. Generally, they are faced with stone (the wall "Carnot style"), have defensive protuberances, and galleries which permitted counter-attacks. Some were destroyed in the Napoleonic period, to be rebuilt, in earth, by the Austrians.

The Military Hospital - Built on the site of the old monastery of Santo Spirito, it was designed to be bomb proof, given

Porta Palio - (Palio Gate), from the race held here. The "Palio" was a length of cloth, crimson for horsemen, green for foot-runners, awarded the winner of the races. Cited by Dante, in his Inferno (it is used as a simile for the eternal chase of the Sodomites), the race originally had the purpose of keeping soldiers in form, and allowing them to show-off their ability. However, its Spartan intent seems to have been lost along the way. In 1393, a women's heat was introduced. Honest matrons refused to participate, objecting to the

Above left: Monument to the Fallen of Cephalonia;
Above: Porta Palio (Palio Gate);
Left: Particular of the walls.

stonework, and classical friezes which continue inside. Once again, Sanmichieli widened and straightened the road leading to the centre. In the Venetian period the gate had a covering which protected the gunners on top from the weather. In the Austrian period, it ceased to be the major entrance, having been reserved exclusively for military traffic. During the flood of 1882, the doors were blown-up to allow the water to escape.

Porta San Zeno - (gate of St. Zeno), so called for the vicinity of the Church of San Zeno, patron saint of Verona. This too is attributed to Sanmichieli. In effect it is a typical Venetian house (with the addition of a city gate in the middle), in which the guardsmen lived as well as worked. Today, it is the office of the "Bacanal" which organises the Carnival, and, in particular, the typical Veronese Carneval figure: the *Papà del Gnocco*. This commemorates the donator of a great quantity of flour, enough to feed the entire area, during a terrible famine. He is immensely fat, has a white beard, carries a gigantic fork, and distributes gnocchi.

Fort of San Procolo - With the continual development of war techniques, the bastions were no longer sufficient. A series of external forts were built, along with, a little later, a further line of defence even further out.

On the polygon of San Procolo were executed those high-ranking fascists, including his son-in-law, who had voted Mussolini out of power.

The Torre della Catena (Tower of the Chain), so called because a chain (14th century) here obstructed the passage of enemy boats, and made it more difficult for merchandise to enter without paying duties. Under Napoleon, after the Easter uprising, the chain was removed and its defences dismantled.

Porta Fura - one of the most representative gates, in as much as, although dating from the Scala period, the successive Venetian and Austrian modifications are visible.

Corso Porta Palio - The street going from Palio Gate towards the city centre

Below: Porta San Zeno (St. Zeno Gate).

22

of the "Scalzi" (shoe-less), so known because of this peculiarity in the dress of its monks. Of the 17th century, by Pozzo, it is dedicated to St.Theresa, and has above the main altar a fine Annunciation by Antonio Balestra. In the Napoleonic period it became a prison.

During WWII many partisans were held here. In addition, those high-ranking Fascists who had voted Mussolini out of his leadership role, during the re-established, north Italian, Fascist "Republic of Salò" (with its ministers in Verona and Milan) here awaited trial and execution.

Palazzo Orti-Manara, by Luigi Trezza, at No.31, is interesting for its four massive caryatids supporting a balcony.

is called "Corso" Porta Palio, where "corso" stands for "race". As a matter of fact, the Palio was run here. It was the Postumius road, built in 147 b.C. by the Roman consul Albinus Postumius. It was one of the longest Roman roads, and connected Genoa with Illyria, passing the Slovenian city of Postojna which still keeps this name. The Via Postumia (Postumius Road) met the Via Gallica at the Gavi arch. Recent excavations have brought to light paving of the ancient street, just below. The road was also called "Via dei Sepolcri" (the Road of Tombs). It was in fact a Roman burial ground.

The Church of the Scalzi - In Corso Porta Palio, there is the Church

Above: Tower of the "Catena" (Chain);
Below: Porta Fura (Fura Gate).

THE CHURCH OF SAN BERNARDINO DA SIENA

In 1450 the Franciscan Bernard, one of the most influential preachers on the Italian scene, was declared Saint. Having preached often in Verona, the people donated a lot known as "la fornase", because bricks were fired here, for a monastery in his honour. Funded exclusively by donations from the city's faithful, work proceeded painfully slowly. The monastery was confiscated under Napoleon, and under the Italians shortly after Unification. In both cases it was rebought by the Franciscans only to be largely destroyed in the bombardments of WWII.

Inside - In Gothic style, it has a single nave to make preaching easier (the side nave, with its private chapels, is a later amplification), with the wooden beams adopted by the Franciscans to emphasise simplicity. Around the bottom of the beams there is a frieze in which one finds the recurring Veronese floral motif, with, at regular

intervals, the monogram of Christ. The *pulpit* and *organ*, its doors painted by Morone, are of the 1400s. On this wall there are two altars: the first, oddly (the Franciscans had begun to emphasise Christ's Passion), a Nativity by India; the second, Baroque, by Bibiena, has an altar painting by Balestra.

Amongst the family chapels in the side nave the followings are of artistic note. The first, frescoed by Giolfino (1522) with the lives of St. Francis of Assisi, and St John The Evangelist. In the fourth there are traces of frescoes by Domenico Morone,and sculptures of the Franciscans Sts. Anthony of Padua, Francis, and Bernard. The fifth has a Crusifixion by Morone and scenes from The Passion by Morando (copy). On the side to the left, by Caroto,

there is an encounter between Christ and Mary, while The Resurection of Lazzarus is by Badile. The other canvases (Capture of Christ, Christ before Pilate, Christ Nailed to the Cross, and a Resurection) are by Giolfino. In a niche there is a 15th century Lament Over The Dead Christ. <u>The sixth</u> is a jewel of Renaissance architecture by San-

michele.
The altar-piece, by India, represents the Christ-child, Mary, and her mother St Anne. In the lunette there is a later Eternal Father by Ottino.
In the Monastery area there remains the Library Room (**Sala Morone**), entirely frescoed by Morone between

1494 and 1503. On the far wall, there are the donators presented to The Virgin, Sts Francis and Chiara, and other Franciscan Saints and Martyrs. The

backdrop, with blue in dominance, represents Lake Garda and Malcesine. On the side walls are represented Franciscan Cardinals and Doctors, who seem to discuss amongst themselves. Above the entrance there are Franciscan Popes.

Austrian powder – magazine - Going from San Bernardino towards San Zeno, on the left, we can see a petrol station which was, in the Austrian period, a powder-magazine, protected by a Faraday cage. The Austrian used telegraph and light signals to communicate among the various fortifications around the city. In Verona they also used, for the first time, the Faraday cage to prevent lightning hitting the magazines. (In the 18th century lightning had hit a Venetian powder magazine of S. Francis, destroying the tower and a vast surrounding zone).

On page 24: The Church of St. Bernardino: façade and entrance;

Above and Left: Detail and View of the "Sala Morone" (Morone Room).

THE CHURCH OF SAN ZENO

The area was a Roman cemetery zone and many sarcophagi and epigraphs have come to light here. One records the lament of a young wife for her Gladiator husband, slain in the Arena. One grave is popularly held to be that of Pipin, Charlemagne's son. Many of the city's first Bishops were also buried here. The eighth (360AD), Zeno, became Verona's Patron Saint. Known as the "Moro" (Dark), for his African descent, he fished, preached, performed miracles (recounted on and around the doors of his church) and fiercely combated the last embers of Paganism. Therefore, he, and his relics, merited a church all their own. The church was ruined and rebuilt a number of times, becoming, in the mean-while, a Benedictine monastery. The present Romanesque Basilica dates from the X century, enlarged and repaired after the earthquake of 1117 (as recorded in a plaque on the side). Far from the heart, it was nonetheless the city's soul. The "Carroccio", chariot symbol of civic pride, independence and liberty, was kept and blessed here. St. Zeno's relics were certain to guard the city's fortunes. One of the first trade fairs of the area was held here. The Emperors of Germany held assemblies in the Monastery. Famous personages stayed in it, it is mentioned by Dante in a passage of his Purgatory; the Venetian administrators celebrated their entrance into the city here.

Transformed in warehouse for the tribute due to the Venetian absentee Abbot, the Monastery was eventually suppressed. Sold under Napoleon, it was used as a quarry for building materials.

Façade - Of the XII century, the Prothyrum (porch) concentrates the decorative message on those entering. Still, the façade is intended to prepare those approaching, as though it were coming into focus: candid golden reflexes; the structure emphasised by the pilasters at the extremes, and those dividing the naves; the lighter pilaster strips which (vertically) with the arches (horizontally) create proportional rhythms in which the decoration is inserted; the fine detailing under the overhang of side naves, which takes up the relieves on the arch and around the window; the gigantic rose window which, with the panels on either side of the Prothyrum, concentrates attention on the centre and the mind on the focal point of the church, the altar.

Finally, one comes to rest before the door, and glances up at the window. This is the work of a certain maestro Brioloto, and depicts a <u>Wheel of Fortune</u>. In the external circle there is a figure who rises

Right: Entrance of St. Zeno;
Below: Mantegna, Tryptic inside St. Zeno.

and falls: sometimes he's up, sometimes down, depending on how the wheel turns. This intriguing representation is not uncommon, even if it seems to have little to do with Christian ideas of Salvation or individual choice. Beneath, and to the right, there is a parenthesis in relief, which shows the Abbot Gerardo offering the church to Christ and the Madonna.

The relieves beside the doors are less ambiguous. Ignoring the lowest panels, the action begins at the bottom and proceeds upwards. On our right, by Niccolò, there are stories from the Old Testament (Creation of the animals, of Adam, of Eve from Adam's rib, Adam and Eve eating the forbidden fruit, the Two expelled from Eden, Adam working and Eve suckling her children). On our left, by Guglielmo, the New Testament (Annunciation, Visit of Mary to Elisabeth, Birth of Christ, Circumcision, Visit of The Magi, Flight into Egypt, Baptism of Christ, Betrayal of Judah and Crucifixion). Interesting the two different

artistic visions expressed by these two contemporaries. The four lowest belong to a previous cycle. Those on our left represent a duel, on the right a hunt.

They refer to Theodoric King of the Goths. The duel (the outcome of a duel is an expression of God's choice) is his conquest of Odoacre King of the Eruli. Having invaded a Roman Italy previously conquered by the Eruli, Theodoric chased Odoacre's armies from one end to the other. After the three year siege of Ravenna he invited Odoacre to a banquet, and killed him. The hunt shows Theodoric obsessed with the capture of a stag, in reality the Devil, which leads him high and low before both leap into the crater of a volcano (hell). Medieval Christianity would have reserved strong doubts about the salvation of his soul: Christian but not Catholic, at the end of his life, suspicious of the loyalty of his Catholic Roman advisors he had a number, including the famous Boetius, executed.

The prothyrum is supported by lions, symbolic guardians of the church. In

the keystone of the arch there is The Lamb of God (Christ and his sacrifice) with the hand of God above. On the sides there are Sts. John The Baptist, and John The Evangelist. In the lunette, at the centre there is St. Zeno, a devil beneath his feet, on his right the merchant class, on his left knights. Both classes sport banners of Verona: a golden cross on azure ground, adopted after their participation in the crusades. This participation is a justification of civic liberty.

In the lower section, in eight little arches, there are three miracles of San Zeno: two ambassadors (1st and 2nd) ask help for the possessed daughter of the noble Gallienus; Zeno gives the two two fishes, but they, seeing a larger one, steal this; when they come to cook, it comes back to life (3rd), they repent returning it to Zeno (4th); Zeno exorcises the demon (5th and 6th); finally, he manages to stop a cart drawn by mad oxen, saving its driver (7th and 8th).

Around the base of the arch there are typical Benedictine representations of work, divided in a calendar: (from the right, outside) March, first month of the year, represented by wind; April gathers flowers; May goes to war; June gathers fruit; July harvests grain; August makes wine barrels; September makes wine; October feeds pigs; November slaughters them; December gathers wood; January warms itself before the fire; February prunes the vines.

The Doors, these bronze panels fixed on wood, no longer follow sequence or scheme, but include biblical stories and miracles of San Zeno. They are the work of at least three masters of different

Above: The Rose-window;
Left: The bell-tower.

periods. The figures in those of the XI century emerge in full relief, those of the XII tend to be flatter. Notable the masks in origin used to open the doors (today missing their rings): a leonine head, and a human-like head with evil words entering the ears in the form of snakes, and leaving the mouth in the form of a Devil. The smaller panels, on the internal margin, represent Saints, Prophets and the four Cardinal Virtues.

In the **bell-tower**, there remains one of the old bells. Known as "del figàr", it rang only during tempests, to ward off hail.

Of the antique splendour of the monastery little remains, apart from a cloister and a **defensive tower** on the left of the church's facade. This however, contains intriguing frescoes which represent a pageant of Knights and exotic animals paying homage to a King figure.

One enters the church by way of **the cloister**, with rounded arches on two sides and pointed arches on the other two, marking the passage from Romanesque to Gothic.

Inside - Its three naves are divided by alternating columns and cross-shaped pilasters. Everything points towards the altar, raised and distant from the body of the church, leaving room for the crypt where the relics were kept. The threefold division is probably a reference to the trinity. The whole is covered by a magnificent Gothic keel roof. Near the

entrance, a monolithic porfiry basin from the Roman baths, originally outside, marked the presence of the Devil. Legend has it that the scrapes were left by the Evil One, defeated by Zeno, and obliged to carry it to his church. It would have excited wonder in the XI century, given that the Egyptian sources of the material had dried up, and the techniques for its working been lost. It now occupies the space of the chariot which carried the symbols of the free city into battle.

Opposite, an octagonal (from the eighth, eternal, day) full-immersion baptismal font of 1194. In this period baptism had become essential, and the right to perform the sacrament was conceded in any church. By Brioloto, the decoration takes up that of the church facade. The Crucifix is of the XIV century.

Down this nave, the frescoes are generally votive, and date from the XIII to the XV century. One notes the over-size St. Christopher. He protected against unexpected sudden death and therefore has to be seen from afar.

The crypt contains the relics of Zeno, dressed as Bishop, and a forest of columns, some of Roman origin, some of Romanesque, each different. There are also the bases of the columns of the upper church.

At the beginning of the **altar area** there is a barrier surmounted by statues of the early 13th century: twelve Apostles and Christ in the centre. Here there are frescoes of the XIII century, amongst which there is the discovery of Zeno's relics. The graffiti on these record important events, such as an invasion,

Above: The cloister.

29

and the nationality of pilgrims who have visited here.

Before the main altar there is the celebrated triptych by Mantegna, representing The Virgin and Christ-child amongst Saints. Typically of the Renaissance, it is conceived of as a window on real space. Here however, the classical columns of the frame are absorbed into the room, with the same architecture used as backdrop. Once again typically, the figures, moving in a unified space, can be said to be taking part in a Sacred Conversation. However, typically of Mantegna, the emphasis is on sculptural definition and they are somewhat static and isolated one from the other. Taken by Napoleon, it was given back in an exchange (1815), with the exception of the scenes underneath, here present in a copy.

Behind, the Gothic abside is frescoed by Martino da Verona, with an Annunciation, a Crucifixion and Saints. Finally, one finds the dark skinned statue of Saint Zeno laughing (1300).

Once again in the cloister, steps lead to the ancient **Chapel of Saint Benedict**. It seems that the body of San Zeno reposed here until 807. In fact the form leads one to think of an early Christian funeral chamber.

Above: Statue of St. Zeno;
Right: Church of St. Zeno,
the inside.

THE CHURCH OF SAN PROCOLO

Parish church of the area until 1806, it was originally a cemetery church of the 5th century. Closed and used as a military deposit and forage deposit and at one point even as a cinema under Napoleon, it was restored in the 80s, just before the whole structure collapsed. The organ doors are interesting, as are the excavations which evidence the early Christian church and various strata of tombs from the Roman period to the end of the 1700, when the cemetery was suppressed under Napoleon. Renaissance reliquaries with the relics of four of Verona's first bishops and a lead Roman funeral house can also be seen

THE REGASTE

The term originally indicated the forest of stakes placed in the water here to avoid the entrance of enemies into the city and protect the irrigation system. As a matter of fact, in this area there was a large system of water-scooping machines used to bring water to the nearby fields. These water-scooping machines were already known to the Greeks but began to be used in the western world between the X and XIII century. From the presence of these water-scooping machines the name of the area: "beverara" or "beora-ra" (in Italian connected with drinking water).

The Church of San Zenetto (Little San Zeno) - Interesting little church dedicated to the protector of freshwater fishermen. It contains a cylindrical altar with the portrait of a wife and husband of funerary origin, upon which there's the stone where tradition wants the Saint to sit whiling away the hours fishing.

Above: Rose window of St. Zenetto;
Left: The façade of St. Zenetto.

CASTELVECCHIO

The Castle was originally known as San Martino in Aquaro (moat) because it had enclosed a church of that name (demolished by Napoleon). It became old (vecchio) only after the construction of new fortifications on the hill of San Pietro. It marks a mile-stone in the fortunes of the Scala family. In 1354 Cangrande II, threatened by insurrections and rival families, having lost a degree of popular consent, and more concerned with consolidation than conquest in the whole of his realm, decided to move his residence from his power base in the heart of the city to a defendable area on the outskirts. By the river, and continuous with the XII century walls (the point where they joined can be seen outside), this position

On pages 32,33 and on these pages: particulars and view of the bridge of Castelvecchio.

During WWII the castle was sight of the trial of Ciano, son-in-law of Mussolini, accused of having betrayed the Fascist cause. He was executed just upstream.

A little later it was bombarded, and the bridge destroyed by the retreating Germans.

Rebuilt as it had been, using the original materials where possible, it was further altered in 1958 by Carlo Scarpa.

He underlined the later construction of the barracks by separating it from the controlling tower and the XII century walls, and redug a moat. It was he who inserted the fountain and water courses which lead to the museum; not simply decorative this isolates from the military area and indicates the museum's intention of slaking the soul's thirst. Scarpa was the first to leave modern materials obvious in restorations, thus marking difference in period and rendering the intervention less invasive.

allowed reinforcement from beyond the city, or flight, or the possibility of dividing the city in two.

The XII century walls also divided the building: the soldier's courtyard, then open to the river, and the Scala residence with the bridge and controlling tower. The bridge opened an escape route towards Germany. It was by way of this that they eventually fled, continuing the family saga north of the Alps. Successively, the castle became stronghold of all dominators in turn. Napoleon constructed a barracks in the courtyard, closing it to the river, the other bank being Austrian territory.

After WWI, part on the castle became a museum. Restored, it was at this point that beautiful doors and windows from destroyed buildings were inserted in the walls of the barracks.

Above and Right: Castelvecchio and its bridge;

On page 37: the drawbridges and the clock tower of Castelvecchio.

on the contrary, the colour is given by the different sands used for the plaster, but milk has been added to those sands to make it more resistant and homogenous and to make it seem antique. Certain parts of the castle have been left open to view, while the view to modern buildings has been hidden by shielding parts of the windows. The original equestrian statue of Cangrande, in origin part of his sarcophagus, is situated in the centre of the route. Visible from various angles and in all its detail, it is positioned on the outside but covered as was originally planned.

As for the museum, there are audio-guides, and each part is furnished with explanation cards. This therefore is intended as an introduction.

The Museum - Interesting are the glimpses one has of military architecture and the decoration of the Scala palace, while Scarpa's restorations has a fascination all its own. The pavements, both those in cement on the first floor and those of the residential palace in walnut, are formed with pieces of different lengths and widths, to avoid repetition. In the Napoleonic barracks the walls are in shining plaster and the colour of the ceiling of the last rooms recalls the colour of the paintings there contained. In the residential palace,

Above: Window partially shaded by Carlo Scarpa;
Above right: Equestrian Statue of Cangrande;
Bottom: Internal Courtyard.

The museum contains works of, or present in, Verona, and has a more or less chronological organisation which concentrates on sculpture in the first rooms passing to painting.

In room 1 there are two relic cases. It is hard to over-emphasise the importance of relics. They were a stimulus to travel (the presence of a relic was often sufficient reason for a journey, or a deviation in a pilgrimage to a more important site) and the consequent exchange of ideas. The fates of monasteries could be determined by the presence of an important relic, in a period when these were the custodians of culture. Even the fates of Empire could be influenced; ie., the transfer of the Magi from Milan to Cologne under Frederick Barbarossa, or the oil with which the Kings of France were anointed. Moreover, the site of a trade fair was usually determined by the festival of a Saint whose relics drew crowds. They were a visible, real presence of and link with Heaven. Hence the care lavished on their containers, which were often great works of art. The two examples here illustrate changes in iconography. The earliest (V century), has representations of cocks (Resurrection) and peacocks (Eternal Life). The other (1179) emblematic moments of the lives of Sts. Sergio and Bacco: their obstinate faith in the True God and the martyrdom suffered for its sake, along with a representation of the Abbot who offered the work, presented by the Saints, and perhaps by merit of the Saints, to God.

Above: Reliquary case of Sts. Sergio and Bacco;
Left: Reliquary case.

14th century, for the first time studied in the church of S. Anastasia. As we can see from these statues, the interest of the period lies in the soul, the body remains completely covered by long garments. The only ornaments are the folds of the garments, the hairstyle or the instruments of martyrdom. The statues are made of sandstone and were once painted. St. John the Baptist is here represented older than Jesus, to convey the idea of wisdom. St. Cecilia, patron saint of the musicians, holds a little bellows organ. St. Catherine and St. Bartholomew hold the palm, the instruments of their martyrdom (respectively the wheel and the knife) and the book to indicate they are doctors of the Church. Above all else, the Crucifixion is notable, with its intensely expressive suffering, deformation and all the ills flesh is heir to. There are Nordic influences here, noticeable in the knotted wooden cross which almost seems a continuation or metaphor of

In the following rooms, there are statues by the Master of Saint Anastasia. This is the name given to a style present in Verona during the

Christ. The Crucifixion, representation today inseparable from the idea of a church, was hardly present, in large format, before the eighth century.

Going out the Napoleonic barrack, one finds the "campana del Gardello" a bell from the guard tower of Piazza delle Erbe. Made by Master Jacopo, scion of a dynasty of bell-makers, its date is there to be read (25 July 1370) along with the figure of San Zeno and the ladder of the Scala family. There are then other examples of bells, once again not to be underestimated in their importance. They were difficult to forge, requiring great experience usually acquired in the course of generations. They were extremely costly: obvious therefore their important role in a cash poor society. They regulated the rhythms of the day, marked festivals, called to prayer and to arms. Introduced near Naples in the fourth century, they signal Christianisation, the first moment in which the whole of late Roman society was

Above: "Crucifixion" and "Suffering for the Death of Christ" by the Maestro of St. Anastasia;
Left: Bell of the "Gardello" (Guard Tower);
On page 41, Large photo: original decorations of the residential section; Below: "Battle of the Knights".

willing to be awoken to go to church, and can therefore be thought of as having rung in the Middle-ages.

Entering the Palace section, the real <u>residence of the family</u>, one finds remnants of the <u>original frescoes</u>, most in imitation of fabrics with geometric and floral motifs.

In this section all things connected to the family, together with other works of art, are collected.

A little "<u>treasure</u>": a star of pearls and glazes alongside a lady's belt, of which remain only the pearls, gold, and precious stones, the silk having rotted. <u>Cangrande's sword</u>, and fragments of a fresco from a family Palace depicting a <u>Battle of Knights</u> , together with frescoes which give sanitary advice. Four <u>statues</u> removed from the Scala family graves, and an <u>Incoronation of the Virgin</u> removed from the tomb (before the church of San Fermo) of Fracastoro, doctor to the family.

Returning from the Palace to the Napoleonic barracks, there is one of the true masterpieces of Veronese sculpture, destined to influence art history. First local example of a tradition which would find its Renaissance expression in the works of the Florentines Donatello and Verrochio, respectively in nearby Padua and Venice. Thanks to Scarpa, the Equestrian Statue of Cangrande, can here be seen in all its details, impossible in its original collocation.

The latter rooms provide a review of Veneto painting (14thcentury onwards), in addition to some absolute masterpieces. We can find here works by Turone, (room 11), Stefano da Zevio e Pisanello (room 12), Jacopo Bellini (room 13), Francesco Morone (room 16), Liberale da Verona (room 18), Nicolò Golfino (room 19), Andrea Mantenga (room 20), Paolo Morando also called Cavazzola (room 23), Gerolamo dai Libri (room 24), Paolo Caliari, called Veronese, and Jacopo Robusti, called Tintoretto (room 25), Pasquale Ottino (room 26), Alessandro Turchi (room 28), Luca Giordano e Gianbattista Tiepolo (room 29). The **Madonna of the Rose-garden** by Stefano da Zevio (1430), depicts an ethereal, exquisitely elegant "Madonna in Humility", in a garden enclosed by roses, Saint Catherine of Alexandria (identified by her attributes in the foreground), and attending Angels. The garden, typical motif of courtly culture in this period, is a symbol laden with significance, ie., Heaven, Cloister, Virginity. The peacocks (like the Quail in Pisanello's Madonna) are symbols of eternal life. The architectural element on the left is perhaps a reference to the fountain of eternal youth, common in chivalrous literature. Otherworldly concerns are emphasised by glances and gestures not direct, and an interaction only between the personages and the angels. The space is uncertain because unimportant. Colour is not a property of the physical world, hardly succeeding in defining the extension of the figures, who float in an enveloping spiritual presence. The whole is an intricate interlacing of gorgeous line reminiscent of the garland, or crown (Crown of Thorns, Prize of Martyrdom, Catherine's role as handmaid to the Queen of Heaven), hanging from Catherine's arm.

Above: Veronese (Paolo Caliari) "Deposition";
Left: Mantegna "Holy Family";
Right: Stefano da Verona "Madonna of the Rose-garden".

THE ARSENAL

This was built in an area known as "Campagnola" (little country-side) because, with its Medieval irrigation system, it traditionally provided vegetables for the city.

Dedicated (1861) to the Austrian Emperor Franz Josef, the Arsenal occupied 62,000 square meters, an area which could be doubled. Connected with the barracks of Castelvecchio, the bridge was closed to civilian traffic. Inside the walls, it was here that artillery was stored and repaired. The red and white stripes are a reference to the Veronese tradition. The fountain in front, was originally the soldiers' bath, where they also learned to swim.

THE GAVI ARCH

In the Roman world wealth implied obligations towards the people and State. To the greater glory of their family, and the city, the gens Gavia had funded the construction of the Roman theatre, and the renovation of the aqueduct, thereby gaining the right to be glorified in a monumental entrance to the suburbs growing up outside the city walls. Beneath the niches, there are still the names of the family members celebrated in the

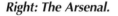

Right: The Arsenal.

statues. During the first century AD, the Roman world was enjoying the Pax Romana, a period of peace which allowed the city no longer to be defined by the limits of its defences. The resulting prosperity, and spirit, was expressed in the adoption of Hellenistic culture, and building on a monumental scale. Unusually, on the inside, the arch is signed. Architecture, for the Romans was not necessarily a prestigious activity, in fact slaves could exercise the profession, and normally their names were not important. Here however, the architect, as indicated, was a freed slave of Vitruvius. Vitruvius was author of ten books on Architecture, which surveyed the entire field, the most famous of the tracts on the subject, and the only one which came down to the Renaissance, and to us. The Arch was incorporated, as a gate, into the twelfth century city walls, occupying a position in the middle of the road before Castelvecchio. Destroyed by Napoleon's troops, to improve the circulation of traffic, the Veronese numbered the pieces, and put aside a sum of money for its reconstruction. This however, took place only in 1932.

Left: The Gavi Arch;
on page 45, Above: Portalupi Palace;
Below: Muselli Palace.

CORSO CAVOUR

From the 1500s many nobles preferred this area, which, following the ancient Via Postumia, was the principal entrance for those arriving from Milan.

Palazzo Canossa - At No.44, is perhaps the most beautiful private edifice to have been built by Sanmichele in Verona. The balcony, a later addition, with statues of a dog with a bone in its mouth is a play on the name Can(dog)ossa(bone). Still today, it is inhabited by members of the ancient Canossa family, whose exemplars include Matilde, famous for her collaboration in Pope Gregory VII's 11th century reform of the Church, and her role in the humbling of Emperor Henry IV.

The main hall was frescoed by Tiepolo. These frescoes, however, were lost in the bombing of WWII. During The Congress of Verona (1822) Tzar Nicholas I resided here.

Palazzo Muselli - at No. 42, XVII century, with a Neo-Classical façade by Pompei and three chimneys in the form of a castle.

Palazzo Portalupi - at No.38, was built by Pinter in Neo-Classical style (1802).

Palazzo Balladoro - at No. 41, designed by Trezza in the second half of the VIII century.

Palazzo Bevilacqua -at No.19, is also by Sanmichele. It remained unfinished, as can be seen in the doors non-central position. The ground floor is in rusticated stonework, with arches on whose keystones Roman Emperors are represented. Unlike the Canossa house, Sanmicheli seems to have been inspired here by the nearby Porta Borsari.

Palazzo Medici - at No. 10, is in Venetian Gothic style, with the series of a-symmetrically positioned grand windows.

The Church of San Lorenzo (St. Lawrence) - Built on the site of the fortified Roman post station. The left tower, with Roman decoration at its base, is what remains of it (towers on the façade are unusual in local religious architecture. Moreover, the towers have castle-like windows, suggesting that the original edifice inspired these.)

Given that the first mention of the church is 9th century, and that it was rebuilt in the XI, we may have a singular example of continuity.

One enters through a gate surmounted by a statue of Saint Lawrence, with the barbeque on which he was roasted alive. Ahead is the Renaissance side entrance, with fragments of the 9th century church all around.

The façade instead is round to the left. The suggestive interior, today with the red and white stripes uncovered by plaster, is unusual for the presence of an upper gallery where women were segregated.

The external towers contain stairs

Below: Bevilacqua Palace;
Right: The towers of San Lorenzo church (St. Laurence).

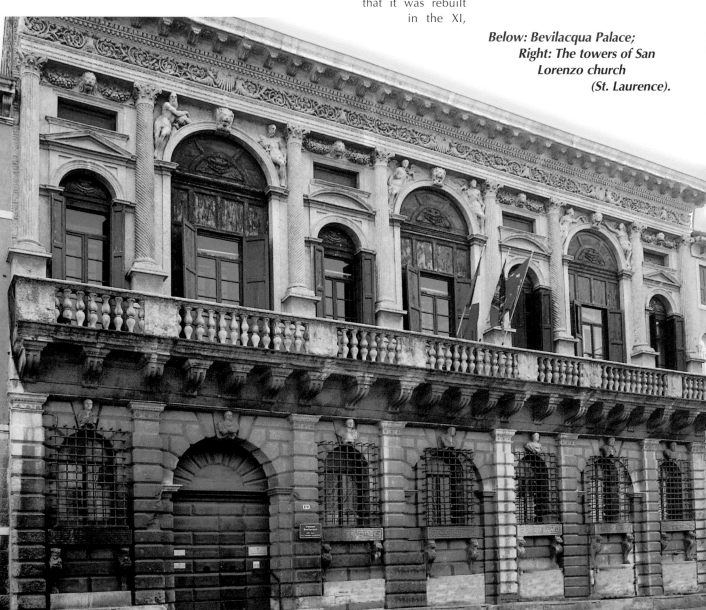

which lead to these.

The church of Santi Apostoli (Holy Apostles) - This suggestive complex dates back to the V century. Parts of the original church are still present in the foundations of the apse.

The church of Sante Teuteria e Tosca (Sts, Teuteria and Tosca) - The church of Sts. Teuteria and Tosca has a Greek cross form (the four arms of equal length), and is collocated at the apse of the Holy Apostles, both characteristics of early churches of

Above and Right: Church of San Lorenzo (St. Laurence), the inside and the entrance.

the Martyrs. Originally, the church was dedicated to St. Apollinaire, dear to the Byzantines, and therefore inimical (an enemy Saint) to the Goths and Lombards. Hence, the dedication was changed. The complex later became the funeral chapel of the Bevilacqua family.

St Teuteria was the daughter of a Noble Englishman. Attempting desperately to flee the attentions of the pagan Osvald, she took refuge here in a grotto where Tosca, sister of Verona's Bishop, lived in prayer and contemplation. Immediately, a spider wove a web

Above: The church of Santi Apostoli (Holy Apostles);
Right: The apse.

before the entrance, making it appear uninhabited, thus saving her from Osvald's henchmen.

Palazzo Carlotti - at No.2, is Baroque (1665).

Palazzo Gobetti, - at No.11, with its harmonious 15th century facade and magnificent portal, is today the seat of the Natural History Museum.

House of the Giolfinos - at No.1. A family of great artists, you can still see the remains of the frescoes by Niccolò on the façade.

This is the zone of ***San Michele alla Porta*** (St Michael at the Gate), so named for a 13th century church built on the remains of a temple dedicated to Jupiter.

When, in 1930, the church was demolished to open present-day Via Diaz, the remains of the temple were removed and reconstructed near the Monumental Cemetery. The zone was given over to trade in raw wool, and to the first stages of its working, as is indicated by the capitol with a lamb. Verona was famous for its production of wool clothes, which were exported all over Europe.

This work here was facilitated by the river used to make the presses work, to wash the wool and to transport the raw wool bales. The wool was first woven, then it was boiled in an alkaline liquid,

generally urine (They collected urine from hospitals, barracks, orphanages and monasteries. The urine from monasteries seems to have been particularly prized because more acid) it was matted and hit with mangles, washed, carded and finally cropped and painted with vegetable colours (those coming from India were particularly expensive but more stable).

The Serenelli Palace - in Via Diaz, is constructed using a part of the city walls. It has a fresco attributed to Francesco Morone, and two plaques indicating water levels in the floods of 1868 and 1882.

Above: detail of the capital of the lamb in Via Diaz;
Left: The Giolfinos' house;
Right: Serenelli Palace.

THE CHURCH OF ST EUFEMIA

This church, dedicated to a Byzantine saint, like Saint Anastasia and San Fermo, is extremely large with respect to the city of the time. All were rebuilt in the Scala period. Verona had been excommunicated because a Ghibelline city, and this damaged commerce. The Scala family, trying to renew relation with the Pope, opened the city to the begging orders, endowing them with churches, lands and public money, and supported the fight against heretics, who till then had freely lived in nearby villages (i.e. the Patarins in Sirmione: 117 of them were burnt alive inside the Arena in a single night). The excommunication was finally withdrawn. St. Anastasia was given to the Dominicans, St. Fermo to the Franciscans and St. Eufemia was given to the Augustinians, who wished to begin working among the people, like the Dominicans and the Franciscans. They rebuilt the pre-existing church in Gothic style. However, in St. Anastasia the partial closing of the public road to enlarge the church did not create particular difficulties, since the bridge at the end of the road had already collapsed, while in St. Eufemia it exited not little consternation among the church's neighbours who undid by night what the monks had done by day. Because of its exceptional size it was pressed into use during the Napoleonic wars and the wars of Italian unification. In the brick façade one can note a statue of St. Eufemia on the top and two other statues on the sides of the entrance door. There are also a rose-window and two lateral windows. Two sarcophagus on the sides, the Romanesque one on the right re-used in the VII century. The inside is at single nave, with a finely decorated ceiling (XVIII century).

On the right, in the first altar there is a "Trinity with Saints" by Jacopo Ligozzi. Among the Saints, St. Anthony, founder of the eremitic life (The Augustinians were eremites) and St. Augustine. In the second altar Torbolo is represented by a St. Barbara, patron of the Bombardiers

Right: Church of Santa Eufemia (St. Eufemia), the portal;

On page 53: Church of Santa Eufemia (St. Eufemia), the façade.

(because lightening struck her executioner). In the third altar Brusasorzi painted a Virgin with Christ-child and Saints. In the transept and presbytery, there are frescoes of the 1300s, amongst which there is an Incoronation of the Virgin, attributed to Martino da Verona. In the Spolverini Chapel, frescoes by Francesco Caroto depict Stories from Tobias (painted in 1508 over a former Gothic decoration). The painting of the Archangels is a copy. In the main abside the sarcophagus of Dal Verme, beginning of XV cen., and a Virgin with Child and Apostles by F. Brusasorzi. On the left side of the church, an interesting Mystic Marriage of Saint Catherine by B. India.

PORTA BORSARI

Originally the Jovian Gate, for the vicinity of a temple dedicated to Jupiter, the present appellation derives from the "bursarii", with their "borse"(purses), who collected taxes, on goods and persons entering in the middle ages.

It opens on one of the two major Roman streets (Decumanus Maximus), at the end of the Roman road (Via Postumia) which has brought traffic from the west for two thousand years. The streets on either side rise precipitously, while before and after, the level of the Roman city has been painstakingly maintained to keep the gate in use.

The part visible today is the decoration of a much larger edifice, not simply an opening in the defences, but a defence of one of its weak spots, with quarters for the guards.

In origin flanked by two towers (whose bases have been unearthed under the contiguous palaces), its Corinthian capitals, fluted semi-columns, and tympani, are typical of early Imperial urban re-organisation on monumental lines.

The epigraph in the trabeation replaced an original inscription, and records the rebuilding of the walls, by Gallienus, after the first "barbarian" incursions. Sections of these can be seen nearby, up Via Diaz.

Right: Porta Borsari (Borsari Gate).

CORSO PORTA BORSARI

Moving up the street, on the right, the de-consecrated church of **San Matteo in Cortine**, of antique foundation, now a restaurant. At the corner with Via Catullo, the head of a Gorgon on one side, a Triton and the symbol of the rising sun on the other, part of a reused **Roman funeral monument**. On the opposite palace, remains of frescoes, with a sun clock. At No.32 the so-called "**Stal de le Vecie**" (stall of the old-people), from the relief with Michael, the Virgin, and the Trinity, which were said to resemble elderly persons: of the 1200s it eventually became a stable and Inn for those arriving in city. At the corner of

Via Spada, hidden just inside the entrance of a shop there are the remains of the **Arc of Jupiter Ammone** (II cen.). So called for a bust of this god with his rams horns (now in the Museo Maffeiano) in the keystone. Ammonite fossils are named for their resemblance to him. The arc had four openings on the arriving roads. It was destroyed only relatively recently.

A little further on one finds the first seat of the **Melegatti** company, where Verona's Christmas cake, the Pandoro, was invented. The building can be recognised by the sculpted cakes on top the corner pilasters. Behind these buildings there is the **Ristorante Dodici Apostoli** (12 Apostoli Restaurant), founded at the end of the 1700s by twelve "piassaroti" (vendors from the nearby market). Interesting are the frescoes and the remains of the Roman city visible underneath.

Above:
Ancient walls in Vicolo del Guasto.

Left: The Gorgon in Corso Porta Borsari, part of a Roman funeral monument;
Right: The church of San Matteo in Cortine (St. Matthew at the walls).

The church of San Giovanni in Foro (St. John in Forum) - VIII cen. Dedicated to St. John the Evangelist, its name reminds us that the Roman forum is the nearby Piazza Erbe.

The present entrance is in fact a side entrance. The façade, originally preceded by a narthex (atrium at the entrance of a church from which penitents, or non-baptised persons, followed the services), has been englobed in the house next door. In a period in which building materials represented a massive investment, houses were often built using the sides of churches. The present entrance has a Renaissance portal with statues by

Above: Meridian;
Right: Side of the previous page Roman funeral monument;

On page 57, Detail of the building called "Stal de le Vecie".

Giolfino: Saints John The Evangelist, Peter and Paul martyred in Rome. At the centre there is a Porcupine Rampant, stem of the Prior who paid for the door.
An external sarcophagus has a written memorial to one of the many fires which devastated the area and its mainly wooden houses. Beneath the tomb there is a block of stone which seems to sweat when bad weather is arriving. Tradition has it that, touching a mask in the lower right corner, one's doubts will be resolved. Recent excavations have

revealed that there were prisons underneath the church. Without doubt, St Anthony of Padova, frequent visitor to Verona, would have interceded for, and brought comfort to, the Padovan prisoners captured by Ezzelino da Romano in the wars of the 13th century and kept here. The pavement mosaics are 19th century, based on early Christian ones. The cemetery is on a higher level due to the burying that succeeded during the centuries.

The internal courtyard was the Parish graveyard.

At No.15 the **Rizzardi Palace**, Baroque of the 17th century. Here there is a characteristic **Caffè**, one of the few remaining historical commercial activities, most of the others having been replaced by name-brand shops of international fame. A sign above the arch at the entrance of **Corte Sgarzerie** (**Sgarzerie's courtyard**) reminds us that, in the middle ages, this place

was used for the final stages of wool working, such as the teaselling (garzatura).The Loggia is still the original, built in 1299 by Alberto I Della Scala, where the garments were checked and imprinted. Under all these shops there are the remains of Roman buildings with their mosaicked floors and frescoed walls, and it may often happen that the toilets of some bars or restaurants around here (usually located downstairs) are 2000 year old rooms. For example, excavations for a garage under Corte Sgarzerie brought to light

remains of a Roman temple. Every new discovery allows us to recompose the puzzle of the Roman city and its life. In front of it one finds Vicolo San Marco (Saint Mark's alley), the name comes from an ancient church which has become a series of shops. Among them a winery where the *"elixir of love"* is sold, a liquor which, according to its inventor, if drunk together with one's beloved, ensures the reciprocation of love.
On the wall of *"Trevisani -Lonardi's house"* there are frescoes by

Falconetto representing the glories of ancient Rome. At the end of the alley is the well of the house where the Italian writer Emilio Salgari was born (1863-1911). He wrote more than

On page 58: The sarcophagus; outside the church of San Giovanni in Foro (St. John in Forum), with particulars;
Above: Brusasorzi, "Deposition" in San Giovanni in Foro (St. John in Forum).

100 novels, most of them set in far countries he had never seen. His most famous character was Sandokan, hero of thousands of children all over the world. In the 1960s, many of his novels were made into movies and nearby Lake Garda became the setting for these, so you could see pirates' galleons or Malaysian junks harboured in. The well here is known as *"The well of Love"* and a sad story about two lovers is narrated. The lovers used to meet here every night although the lady's noble parents warned her against her beloved's (of humble origins) intentions.

Not knowing who to believe to, the girl one evening asked her lover to throw himself into the well as a proof of true love. He died and she, realising that his was true love,

conscience stricken, decided to commit suicide. Walking across the archway that leads to Piazza Erbe, one finds at the footstep of a ladder, an ancient stone with the "filetto" game (Merrill). On this stone the Veronese people, in Roman times, used to play with white and black stones.

QUA·FURONO·I·LANIFICII
OND'EBBE·TANTO·LUSTRO·E·POTENZA
IL·VERONESE·COMUNE
DAL·SECOLO·TERZO·AL·QUATTORDICESIMO
DELL'ERA·VOLGARE

Above: Stone with the ancient game called "Tria" (merrills);
Left: Corte Sgarzerie, the writing on the entrance;
Right: The Well of Love.

PIAZZA DELLE ERBE
(The Vegetable Market)

This square was, in every sense, the original centre of the city, and retained its position as fulcrum of civic life throughout the ages. In origin the Roman Forum, at the conjunction of the major NS and EW streets of the Roman grid plan (still largely present), its size was equal to that of two Roman blocks (75 x 150 m). It retains its original length today, while its width is greatly reduced. The most important Roman public buildings were here: the Capitolium (temple of the principal deities) the remains of which are visible under Palazzo Maffei, the Basilica (covered markets), the Curia (government house), and the Comitium (open meeting-place) complete with podium for orators. The whole was surrounded by porticos which also housed markets. The name derives from the vegetable (Erbe) market held here from the XV century.

Today, at the two extremes, one finds columns: one with images of Saints who protect the market; the other, taller, with the **Lion of St. Mark** symbol of Venetian hegemony (without sword and with an open Bible

indicating that Verona allied and was not conquered). Destroyed during the Napoleonic invasion, it was replaced after Italian Unification.

The so-called "**Berlina**", in the middle of the square, was the place where criminals were exposed to public ridicule. Essential in a market-place, on one of the columns there are four length measurements, the regulation size of bricks and roof-slates on the base, and a chain from which hung a measure of capacity.

The **Fountain of Madonna Verona**, (it has come to personify Verona), is composed of a basin from the Roman baths and a Roman statue found nearby. It was placed here in 1368 by the Scala rulers to celebrate their restoration of the city's aqueduct. Hence there is a motto in the statue's hands extolling the virtues of Verona and the justice which reigns in Her dominions. On the base are sculpted heads representing ancient "Kings of Verona".

In the area once occupied by the Roman basilica, in the Comunal period there was a building reserved for the use of the merchants' associations. Here, in 1301 Alberto della Scala built the "**Domus Mercatorum**" (House of Merchants), a long brick building with Guibelline M-shaped battlements, which until recently was seat of the local government trade organisation. Here the merchants organized also classes of Mathematics and German, and from this small beginning the University of Verona sprang up. In the year 1339 the University already had specializations in Law, Medicine and Literature, making it one of the oldest in Italy.

To the left **a statue** commemorates the victims of the first aerial bombardment of Verona, during WW1. Renaissance style palaces follow, with frescoes by Girolamo Dai Libri. In the XVI century Verona's wealthy imitated their richer Venetian peers, decorating their palaces with frescoes. Verona came to be known as "urbs picta" (the painted city).

The **tower of the "Gardello"** (guard tower), whose primary function was that of prison and watch-tower, is also

known as the clock tower for its clock, installed by Cansignorio in 1370: to the greater glory and efficiency of the city, it is the first mechanical example in Verona. Just outside, a cage was hanged, for the sentenced people, as the nearby hotel name recalls. Just behind the Gardello Tower was the "Monte dei Pegni" (Pawnshop/bank), an institution founded to help those in need of money avoid falling into the hands of lone-sharks. Here, jewels or precious garments, etc. could be brought and the owner received an amount proportional to the value of the item, which could, in any moment, be redeemed. Noblemen acted as the warrant. Soon all classes began to use the system, even the Scala family, because banks as such did not exist, and it was therefore a way of protecting precious items. Napoleon confiscated all items, and the pawnshop was closed. Later it burned. Today there remains the clock donated by count Nogarola. However, notoriously inaccurate, the people punned on the count's name rebaptising it "no ga l'ora" (doesn't keep time).

Above: The square with Lamberti Tower and the Townhall of the 12th century;
Left: The Berlina (place of public corporal punishment).

On the sight of the Roman temple (parts of which are visible beneath it), the Baroque XVII century **Palazzo Maffei** crowns the square. On its top, from the left, Hercules, Jupiter, Venus, Mercury, Apollo and Minerva. A previous house here was owned by the mercenary general Gattamelata, immortalised by Donatello, in nearby Padua, in his equestrian statue reminiscent of the Scala arches.

Casa Mazzanti was again frescoed with allegorical figures by Alberto Cavalli (student of Giulio Romano). Not an isolated case, these gigantic figures show how the possibilities of colour and narration sometimes take precedence over the more subdued tendency to have statuary and architecture form a harmonious whole. Nearby a small tower became part of the fortifications of the **Domus Nova** residence of the Podestà (a type of aristocratic policeman employed to keep peace between warring factions). When, under the Venetians, the Podestà was abolished, the building became the house of the judges of the nearby Tribunal.

The arc known as "**Arco della Costa**" (The Arc of the Rib) for the whale rib hanging underneath. This was placed here, in the XV century, by a Pharmacist, who wished to draw attention to his adjacent store. He sold exotic merchandise and spices, from afar just as whales were from afar. The arc is a passage, which allowed, in the Venetian period, the Judges to pass from their residence to the Courts, without risking menaces, or attempts at corruption.

Above: The fountain of "Madonna Verona" and Mazzanti House in the background;
Above: "Arco della Costa" (Arch of the Rib);
Left: Maffei palace.

PIAZZA DEI SIGNORI
(Lords' Square)

Medieval political centre, the square derives its name from the presence of the Scala family's Palaces. It is also known as Piazza Dante for the statue of the same, placed here in 1865 (Dante was a guest of the Scala here). *Palazzo del Comune (city hall) -* known also as Palazzo della Ragione (Palace of Reason) because the Venetians made it their judge's seat. Built in the 12th century in the typical Veronese Romanesque alternation of red and white, on the façade there are symbols of the Venetian government (partially destroyed under Napoleon). There is also a "bocca del leone" (lion's mouth), typical feature of Venetian justice, in which one could place anonymous complaints about lone-sharks. The Judges then investigated. I t

was not necessary that the accused be advised of the process before his imprisonment. There is another around the side, for those who hadn't paid taxes on their silk production. The internal court is known as the "Mercato Vecchio" (Old Market) for a grain market which was here held. It had porticoes to facilitate the circulation of crowds, and the so-called "Scala della Ragione", the fine XV century staircase, that provided access to the courts during the Venetian period. Inside, notable are the frescoes of the Notaries' chapel.

The Lamberti Tower - Built in 864 it was, from the 12th century, a castle house of this family, memory of the internecine faction fighting which w o u l d

have led many families to protect themselves in this manner. Heightened in the XIV, XVI, and XIX centuries, as can be seen from the different styles, its Belfry was added in the 15th century to house Verona's city bells. These regulated the civic life of the city. The Marangona rang in case of fire (in the 12th and 13th centuries the city was still largely in wood) and regulated the working hours of the carpenters (marangoni). The larger bell is known as the Rengo (harangue) because it called to political meetings, or to arms.

Palazzo del Tribunale - With the rise of the Scala's, against city law, these new rulers built their residences in the precincts of government house. These edifices, although open on the lower level to allow public meetings, were connected one to the other on the upper level, and were easily defendable for the presence of towers. Little by little the symbols of Scala power came to be concentrated here, and the family associated with the organs of government, until the building of a new fortified residence, Castel Vecchio, on the outskirts, at the end of their reign. This fortified family palace was built by Alberto Della Scala and then restored by Cansignorio. It then became the seat of the Venetian military governor, and of a school for Bombardiers. Hence, the Bombardiers' gate, the "**Porta dei Bombardieri**", with its references to the military art (1687). During the Austrian domination it became part of the nearby Tribunal and the towers were used as court's prisons. Therefore, it is known as the Palace of the Tribunals,

"Palazzo dei Tribunali". Its internal courtyard is linked to a garden behind, in origin belonging to the Scala family, where Romeo and Juliet probably met. Through this internal courtyard one can enter the "Scavi Scaligeri", excavations of the Roman and Medieval city, partially

visible through the glasses. The area of the excavations, opened in 1996, is very extensive and of particular interest because it allows us to see the evolution of the Roman city, from the epoch of its foundation to the decadence of the late Empire, the Barbarian invasions, the Medieval period, up until the construction of the actual buildings in the Scala period. Of the Roman period there are pavement

On top: "Bocca di Leone" (Lion's mouth) for anonymous denunciations against usurers. On this page, on top: Roman mosaic in the Scaligeri's excavations Above: "Bocca di Leone" (Lion's mouth) for denunciations against silk smuggling. Left: Piazza dei Signori: from the left: "Palazzo dei Tribunali" (Tribunals Palace) with its tower which was used as a prison, "Palazzo del Comune o della Ragione" (City Hall or Reason Palace) with the Lamberti's tower and the Domus Nova (New House).

mosaics amongst which, most interestingly, one from a "triclinium" (dining room). There are paving stones with the sidewalk raised at the sides, and, underneath, lead drains, well made and very well conserved, used for centuries after the end of the Roman period. From the Barbarian period remain Longobard tombs, while from the Medieval period there have been found the remains of food, which have permitted an idea of the Medieval diet: meat was eaten rarely and usually came from courtyard animals, while larger animals - oxen or horses – were eaten only at the end of their working lives. Some surprises have emerged such as the remains of a camel, probably belonging to a Byzantine army.

Palazzo di Cangrande (Cangrande's Palace) - Back in the square, the building with the M-shaped Ghibelline battlements is the main Scala palace. The arc which links it to the Tribunal Palace is said to have had instruments of torture hanging from it, a warning to the people. The façade instead is fruit of a dubious attempt to restore its original aspect: with the aid of a painting in Castelvecchio, subsequent modifications

On page 66: "Porta dei Bombardieri" (Bombardiers Gate);
Above: Cangrande's Palace;
Left: The arch which links the Palace of the Tribunals with Cangrande's Palace, on which it is said, torture instruments were hung as a warning.

were removed, with the exception of the Venetian lion. Its open area corresponds to the political podiums present in other political squares of the period. The internal courtyard has a double portico with the remains of frescoes, and a central well. Many illustrious persons were guests here, including Dante. Despite his association with the Ghelf cause, and the contrasting allegiance of the Scala family to the Ghibellin party, Dante was invited to Verona for the lustre reputation. Likewise Petrarch remained for a time at their court.

Santa Maria Antica (Old St Marys') - There have been churches and convents on the site since the 7th century.

The present church was built after the earthquake of 1117, typically with the Veronese Romanesque alternation of red and white. It became "Old" only after the building of the nearby Santa Maria in Chiavica. With the rise of the Scala, and their creation of a power-base in the area, it became their private chapel, the cloister becoming their burial ground. It is said that, in the crypt, there are dozens of skeletons, some without heads, result perhaps of the suppression of opposition. However, before the advent of the family, this was the cemetery of the area. Amongst those buried inside the church there is a certain Frigotto, whose gravestone explains that, as a symbol of the expiation of his sins, he wanted to be buried in chains.

Of particular importance for the Veronese, there is here, the chapel of Santa Rita, patron of impossible miracles. Amongst the plaques, one records the holding of a Bishops' synod, and it long remained associated with the Bishops.

Scaligero Arcs - Above the lateral access to the church is the **tomb of Cangrande** (1291/1329). Having braved the forces of innumerable cities, conquering almost down to the coast, after hours of bloody battle for Mestre he asked for a glass of water. As soon as he drank the water, given him by an elderly woman, he was taken with stomach pains and died.

The water was perhaps too cold. Carried home, his devoted subjects wished to bury him with the greatest possible honours, choosing therefore an elevated position above the door.

This sarcophagus begins the tradition of the family's monumental tombs. His last resting place is supported by dogs with ladders, and decorated with relieves depicting the Resurrection.

The dog refers to his name (Can), symbol of

On page 68: La "Scala della Ragione" (The Steps of Reason); Above: Scala's Tombs and Cangrande's Palace.

Left: Piazza dei Signori (Lord's Square) at night;
Below: Statue of Dante.

fidelity, and tenaciousness, and to the Mongol Emperors (Khan), widely held to be allies of Christendom in its fight for the reconquest of the Holy Land. Moreover, it seems that his Mother had dreamed of giving birth to a dog, a good omen.

The ladder is a reference to the family name (Scala), in its turn symbol of various types of ascent.

Above, there is an equestrian statue (a copy), reference to the Roman Equestrian statues, and a theme taken up not only in the tombs of his successors but in nearby Padova by Donatello, and in Venice by Verocchio.

At the two corners of the enclosure are the Arcs of Mastino II and Cansignorio.

The *arc of Mastino II* was commissioned

Right: Cansignorio's sarcophagus;
Below: Mastino's II (left) and
Cangrande's (right) sarcophagi.

while he was still alive and able to watch its construction from the adjacent Palace. Above four angels watch over the defunct. There are also reliefs with Genesis and the tree of life.

The **Arc of Cansignorio**, more elaborate than those of his more illustrious forebears, is the work of Bonino da Campione.

It contains statues of Warrior Saints, Angels and Virtues, and reliefs with biblical themes. One hoof of the equestrian statue is supported by an Evangelist.

Finally, within the wrought-iron enclosure (original) are five simple graves of Scala family members. The raised graves, in contrast, become increasingly elaborate with the passage of the 14th century, charting the development of the Gothic: from the Simple Gothic prototype of Cangrande, to the Flaming Gothic tomb of Mastino II, through to the International Gothic of Cansignorio's monument.

The "Loggia di Fra' Giocondo", named after its presumed architect, can be seen going back to the square. In the XV cen.

Verona had been definitively deprived of its independence by Venice and the former town hall had become the Venetian courtrooms, so this building was built to house the remaining organs of self-government, and it is almost as if it provided a new means of nostalgically recalling the city's grandeur.

One of the first purely Renaissance constructions here, it reminds us of Verona's importance in the Roman Empire. The statues represent illustrious Roman Veronese: (from the left)Vitruvius, Catullus,

Pliny, Cornelius Nepote, and Macrus. On the facade one also finds representations of Roman Emperors and symbols of the city.

In this page, La "Loggia di Fra' Giocondo" and Cangrande's Palace in Piazza dei Signori (Lords' Square).

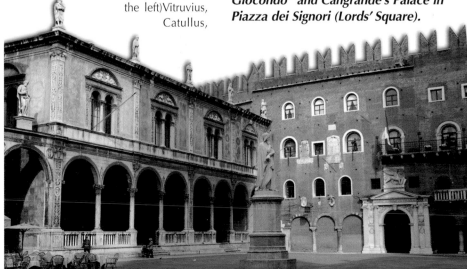

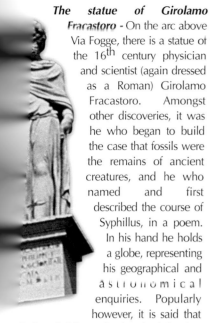

The statue of Girolamo Fracastoro - On the arc above Via Fogge, there is a statue of the 16th century physician and scientist (again dressed as a Roman) Girolamo Fracastoro. Amongst other discoveries, it was he who began to build the case that fossils were the remains of ancient creatures, and he who named and first described the course of Syphillus, in a poem. In his hand he holds a globe, representing his geographical and astronomical enquiries. Popularly however, it is said that ball will fall on the head of the first ...nest person to walk underneath. The ...tue is of 1559. Under the arc, a narrow ...ey: Via Fogge. It follows, like others, the ...act route of a Roman street. Straight ...rallel alleys of this kind are, in Verona, ...own as "bine", and to be "fora de bina" ...ut of the bina) is to be not quite in one's ...ead.

he "Casa della Pietà" (House of Pity) - It ...ow houses the Caffe Dante, renowned ...om the 1800s as a literary and artistic ...lon. Here were to be found papers in all ...anguages. Originally Caffe Squarzoni, it ...ssumed its present title when, in 1865, the statue of Dante was erected in the square before it. However, the grounds were originally occupied by one of Verona's orphanages.

A certain Taddea da Carrara, wife of a Scala, struck by the sad sort of abandoned children, particularly the girls who usually finished as prostitutes, donated these precincts. Here boys learned a trade, girls were provided with a small dowry.

Volto Barbaro - Is the passage between the House of Pity and the Domus Nova. It leads behind the Mazzanti houses, where there is an ancient well, in which one can still see the system used to transport water to the surrounding inhabitations.

It was here that Mastino della Scala was murdered. To avenge the fact, Alberto his brother requested emergency powers, never afterwards renounced. This spot marks the beginning of the Scala reign. Here as well, began the "Pasque Veronesi" (Veronese Easter) the uprising against Napoleon's troops in 1798.

CORSO SANTA ANASTASIA

This road follows the Roman decumanus maximus which at that time reached the Adige and the Postumius bridge. The name "corso" (race) was given to the major internal roads in which the Palio was run. At the corner with via Rosa there is a **Roman plague** which records how the Gavi family donated a massive sum towards the building of an aqueduct. At the corner with vicolo Cavalletto there is a late **Gothic altar** dedicated to the Madonna. At number 38 there is **Casa Bevilacqua** where judge Pietro Alighieri lived, son of Dante.

The well inside is worth a look. In Via Forti (a sideway of Corso St.Anastasia), is the **Forti Palace**, today a contemporary art gallery open during exhibitions, many of which of international importance . This complex of buildings were originally the seat of Longobard dukes, becoming, in the XIII century, the seat of Ezzelino da Romano, and then the headquarters of Napoleon during his Italian Campaign. In the 1800s, it was the property of Achille Forti and at his death, for want of heirs, it became a foundation. During restorations Roman period buildings and a road came to light. Oddly enough, the road was not part of the original Roman grid, but was nonetheless large, so it must have led to an important building, probably the thermal baths.

MINISCALCHI MUSEUM

Founded by the last Count of this line, to display the collections amassed by his family throughout the centuries.

On the upper floor there is a rich collection of drawings by the Veronese artists ubiquitous in Verona's churches, together with Renaissance bronzes by Jacopo Sansovino, amongst others. Impressive the collection of armaments from the mid 14 to the early 1600s, and the archeological collection of Roman, Etruscan, and Italic pieces. Finally, a room is dedicated to Ludovico Moscardo, 16th century eccentric whose Wunderkamer gave a great impulse to scientific collectionism.

On page 74 top left: Statue of Gerolamo Fracastoro;
Below: The plaque in Volto Barbaro.

MASTINO I DELLA SCALA ELETTO PODESTÁ NEL 1259 CAPITANO DEL POPOLO NEL 1261 CADDE UCCISO A TRADIMENTO PER ODIO PRIVATO LI 26 OTTOBRE 1277 PRESSO QUESTO VOLTO

THE CATHEDRAL OF VERONA: SAINT MARY MATRICOLAR

The Devil is always present outside the most important churches. On the side porch, and in a sarcophagus on the opposite side, one finds odd indentations. These stones release sulphur, the stink of Hell, when struck with a stone. Generations of children have meditated on Virtue and the After-life doing just that. Otherwise only its size announces the importance of the Cathedral ("Cattedra", throne of the Bishop). It seems to be in the wrong part of the city. Religious centre by definition, religious it may be, centre it is not. Far from the fulcrum of civic life, it is in fact crammed into the furthest periphery of the old city. Cathedrals often occupy positions just inside the Roman walls. They were inserted as an afterthought, and had to coexist for a time with previous structures. During the

"barbarian" invasions however, they became essential, Church authority coming to substitute the apparatus of the Roman state. In fact, many titles used in the Catholic hierarchy, and the names of its administrative divisions, are taken wholesale from the late Roman Empire. Moreover, as the middle-ages advanced, and the population became almost exclusively rural, cities became little more than administrative centres for a Diocese, with the Bishop's presence the reason for the city's continued existence.

After 1000, the rebirth of urban society generally recognised this role as cultural pole, new suburbs springing up around the new centre. With the river and the hill behind, this was not possible here. Moreover, the centre of civic pride

Top left: mosaics of the early Christian Basilica;
Below: Cloister of the Canons' chapter;
Right: Church of St. Helen, the façade.

became San Zeno Therefore, one has to look round-about the Cathedral to imagine its importance.

Behind, there is the **Bishop's palace**. The present building, largely of the 16th century, contains frescos by Brusasorzi, and, above the gate, is guarded by statues of the Virgin, Sts. Peter and Paul (underling Catholic orthodoxy), and the Archangel Michael (by Giovanni da Verona). However, its inner courtyard contains the tower of Bishop Ognibene (1172). Its battlements are testimony to the Bishop's need for more worldly defence. Much of the area before it, and around, also belonged to the Bishop, it was here that the administrative activities of centuries took place. As for the Cathedral itself a first basilica was built here at the beginning of the 4th century while the mass conversion of Roman society was underway. Already, around 360 AD, the Christian community had burgeoned, and it was rebuilt.

Part of this compex is visible in the **cloister of Sant'Elena** (where tradition holds that Dante recited his works). The pavement one sees was heated, and in the mosaics there are the names of persons who contributed to its construction. It seems that the complex included a second basilica, beneath the present Cathedral, and a Baptistery.

The present edifice was begun after the earthquake of 1117. Romanesque, later remanagements in the 14 and 1500s lent it Gothic and Renaissance characteristics.

Façade - The Romanesque prothyron (porch), before the central door is the focal point, as it would have been even before the façade was heightened and the Gothic windows and guiles added. Niccolò, original architect of the church, is here concentrating the decorative message on those entering. The two Griffins stand guard against evil influences. On the front there are the figures of St. John The Baptist and St. John The Evangelist with The Lamb of God (Christ) between. The first, paved Christ's way, the second diffonded His Message.

Below: Inside of the Cathedral;
Right: Bishop's residence, entrance.

79

Around the door there are various Prophets, with prophecies regarding Christ and Mary, and before them, Charlemagne's Paladins, Orland and Oliver, testimony to the popularity of chivalrous literature, the idea that the Gospel could be defended with the sword, and the prestige of Charlemagne (for some a Saint) first Holy Roman Emperor. Above there are the symbols of the four canonical Evangelists, and, in the lunette, Mary with the poor Shepard, and the rich Magi. Beneath Mary there are the three theological virtues: Faith, Hope and Charity.

The Romanesque apse is intact. From the same period all around there are fragments of friezes with

vegetable and animal motifs, and a lateral entrance with representations of Jonah swallowed by the whale (perhaps a reference to the Resurrection) and a dog biting a lion.

Inside - The Gothic columns and crossed vaults set the architectural tone. However the sense of horizontal space rather than upwards movement, combined with the pictorial decoration, particularly the trompe l'oile around the side altars, lend it a Renaissance flavour. The stone frameworks and statues at the summits of the side altars belie their late Gothic origin. Amongst the paintings in these there is an "Assumption of The Virgin" by Titian (first on

the left), an "Adoration of the Magi" by Liberale da Verona with a "Deposition" by Giolfino (second on the right), and a "Transfiguration" by Cignaroli (third on the right). The last altar on the right, in a Gothic baldaquin, contains relics of Saint Agatha, an early Christian martyr from Sicily who refused the advances of a Roman Consul, refused to sacrifice to the Roman Gods and had her breasts ripped off in consequence (particularly popular in painting). Before the main altar there is a barrier designed by Sanmichele. Behind one can see frescoes executed by Torbolo on designs by Giulio Romano, reminiscent of his Room of The Giants in Palazzo Te (Mantova). A door on the left leads to the church of **San Giovanni in Fonte** (Saint John of the Font) where there is the Baptismal Font. Octagonal (the eighth day of creation which represents eternity), it is from the XII century by the school of Brioloto, and has reliefs with salient moments from the family life of Mary and a Baptism of Christ.

MUSEO CANONICALE (The museum of the Canon's Chapter)

Opened in 1988, it contains **sculptures** dating from the XII to the XV cent., precious **wood paintings** of the 14 and 1500s and **oil on canvas** of the 15 and 1600s. Most of the works of art come from the Cathedral and the previous churches of the area.

BIBLIOTECA CAPITOLARE (The Library of the Canon's Chapter)

On the left of the Cathedral square, it's the oldest surviving library of Europe. Founded in the fifth century, one of the main figures of Humanism, Petrarch, was unearthing classical documents here a thousand years later (XIV century). It's famous all over the world for its precious **illuminated codexes and anthem books**, among which the oldest writing in the Italian language. It also preserves **paintings** by famous painters, **sculptures**, **coins**, and a precious collection of **ancient musical instruments**.

Top left: apse with the choir enclosure by Michele Sanmichieli.
Left: San Giovanni in Fonte, the Baptistery;
Above: Titian "The Assumption".

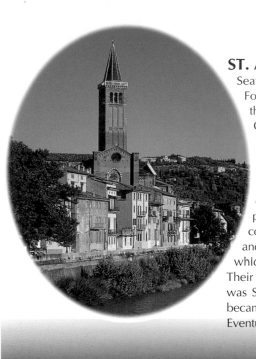

ST. ANASTASIA

Seat of the Domenican monks. Founded by St Dominic (begining of the 13th century), these hounds of God (a pun on their name, "Dominis Canis") had the task of sniffing out heresy, fighting it by the example of their lives (upright in contrast with those of the corrupt clergy), through their preaching and preparation in theology (again contrasting with that of the clergy), and by any other means necessary, which included staffing the Inquisition. Their most celebrated Veronese exponent was St Peter Martyr: son of heretics, he became a ferocious persecutors of heresy. Eventually ambushed and martyred by his enemies, representations of him, with a knife implanted in his skull, in many cities, for the next couple of hundred years, are testimony to this struggle and his importance. When (second half of the 13th century), the Dominicans moved inside the city, fulfilling their mandate of working and preaching amongst the people, they received two churches close together: St Anastasia (originally not a saint but an Icon), and St Remigio. After St. Peter Martyr's death, they demolished these, to erect another larger, dedicating it to him. However, the people continued to call it St. Anastasia. Begun in 1290 with contributions from the Scala family and their allies, work continued piecemeal for the whole of the 13 and 14

hundreds. Consecrated in 1471, in reality work continued into the 1500s. The façade hasn't been finished yet. Despite the cultural changes during this period, the church is pre-eminently Gothic.

Façade - The Gothic door-way with its red, white and black stripes (these latter two corresponding to the Dominican habits) is surmounted by scenes from Christ's life. At the extremes of the architrave, St. Anastasia (left) and St. Catherine of Alexandria (right). A statue of Mary with the Christ-child adorns the summit of the central pilaster, on which are incised St. Peter Martyr (left), St. Dominic (centre), and St. Thomas Aquinas (right). Beneath these, there are in order a sun, a star, and a moon,

attributes of the three. In the lunette there is a badly damaged fresco, attributed to Badile, representing the Trinity with the people below, in adoration, led by the Saints. In the Renaissance panels to the sides of the portal (two were never given back after Napoleon took them) there is a martyrdom of St. Peter Martyr, and a miracle of the cloud which lends shade while St. Peter Martyr preaches. The prominence given to windows is in keeping with the Gothic emphasis on light. ***Inside -*** Its bones and spirit are Gothic. The crossed vaults and pointed arcs should clash with the later Renaissance side chapels. Instead, these seem in keeping with the Gothic tendency to have wall space disappear. Moreover, the crossed vaults were eventually frescoed with a floral motif, making the simple columns become, again, a Gothic forest. At the entrance one is offered holy water by two figures which may represent beggars (reference to the Dominicans, a begging order), or mill workers from the nearby mills. Their extreme fatigue in supporting the basins, has led them, traditionally, to be called hunchbacks. The one on the right is by Veronese's father. Typically of Domenican churches, there are five apses. On the far right, the **Cavalli**

funerary chapel. Here there are frescoes (around 1370) by <u>Altichiero</u>: a knight presented to the Virgin Mary by a warrior Saint. This is the first work attributed with any certainty to him. Typically, the sense of space, if not profound, given the defining limits of curtains and throne, is filled to bursting. Slow, solemn rhythms vie with touches of lively realism. Soft colour, warm light. The sarcophagus lunette (early 1400s) instead, is by Stefano da Zevio. Other frescoes by the local school represent a Virgin with the Christ-child, a St. Christopher and a Miracle of St. Eligio. On the left there is also a Baptism of Christ by a Bolognese painter. To the left, the **Pellegrini** Chapel, with outside, above the arc, the celebrated fresco <u>St. George and the Princess</u> (1433) by Pisanello. Its attention to naturalistic detail, decoration, and line, typical of chivalrous late Gothic taste, is here exacerbated in a dream-like, irrational atmosphere, in which action and sentiment are suspended in space and time. On the internal walls there are terracotta scenes from the life of Christ by

Top left: foreshortening of the church of St. Anastasia;
Left: Night time view;
Above: inside.

83

Michele da Firenze (1435). On either side, decorating the 14th century sarco-phagi, frescoes by Martino da Verona (right) and Altichiero (left).

On the left hand side of the **main altar** there is the equestrian statue of Cortesia Serego framed by an An-nunciation and Saints, by Giambono. On the right a Last Judgement (mid 1300s) attributed to Turone.

Next on the left, 15th century frescoes which have joined the mainstream of Renaissance culture, but retain a dramatic sense of landscape. The **fifth apse** is the base of the bell-tower. One can see the cords used to ring the bells. On the left, decoration, by Farinati and Morone, around the door to the **Giusti chapel.** Inside, the 15th century wooden stalls in origin found at the main altar, and a Virgin with The Christ-Child and Saints by Felice Brusasorzi. Outside, to the left, there is the **Chapel of The Rosary**, dedicated to The Madonna of The Rosary, responsible, it seems, for the salvation of Venice, in the naval victory of Lepanto (1571) against the Ottoman Turks. At the altar, by Lorenzo Veneziano (14th cen.), a Madonna in Humility with, at her feet, Mastino II of the Scala family and his wife. Above and below there are angels with roses by Orbetto. Other frescoes were added at the beginning of the 17th century. Going down the nave on this side there are two paintings by Nicolò Giolfino and the imposing **Baroque organ** from under which one entered the cloisters.

On the **counter-façade** there is a great canvas portraying The Council of Trent (which gave rise to the Counter-Reform, the Catholic reaction to the Protestant Reformation).

Arc of Guglielmo da Castelbarco - To the left of Saint Anastasia there is the raised tomb of the Scala ally, who having con-tributed to the churches construc-t i o n, wished to be buried beside it. The Arc, r e c a l l i n g m o d e l s f r o m L o m - bardy, is e a r l i e r

Above: holy water holders supported by "hunchbacks"; Below: Pisanello "Saint George and the Princess".

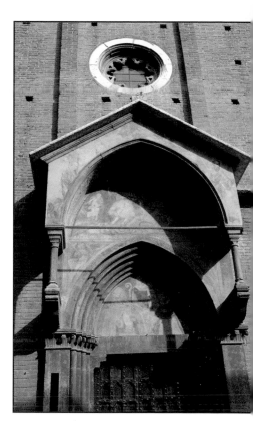

than those of the Scala family. Passing under the Arc one enters the cloisters of the monastery, now a school.

The Church of St. Giorgetto - This is another church which the Dominicans also tried to name St. Peter Martyr but which is still commonly known as St. Giorgetto. St. George in fact was Patron Saint of the German Knights sent in aid of Cangrande II by his Imperial father-in-law, Ludovic of Bavaria. They lodged in the Scala Palace of the Eagle opposite (today the Due Torri Hotel), and prayed in the church. Inside the church there are many stems belonging to these knights. In addition, a fantastic allegorical garden, of the 1500s, by Falconetto, painted on a commission by the occupation forces (German) of Emperor Maximilian.

Left: Guglielmo da Castelbarco's Sarcophagus;
Right: Detail from the Church of San Giorgetto;
Below: Church of St. Anastasia, the baroque organ.

PIAZZETTA BRA' MOLINARI (Little Square at the widening of the Mills)

It's behind the church and its name reminds us that here, the river having widened and the current become swifter, there was a concentration of mills.

LA PESCHERIA VECCHIA (The Old Fish Market)

Down Via Ponte Nuovo (so called because the street led straight onto a bridge new when the Scala family built it) one sees it on the right. Built in the XII cen. to spare customers the tricks of the vendors (such as painting the eyes to make them seem fresher or putting pebbles inside their stomachs to make them weight more).

Beneath: Left: "House of Romeo"; Right: "Piazza delle Poste" (Square of the General Post-office) with Statue of Garibaldi.

VIA SOTTORIVA

Called like this because it was under the level of the river, it's one of the many covered streets of the middle-ages. These had evolved, not simply to provide shelter, but to provide extra exposition space for the workshops (glass windows didn't exist), allowing artisans to pay fewer taxes on the space occupied by their shops. The people preferred walking in this area because it was common usage to throw slops from the windows. The height of the arches were regulated to allow mounted men to pass. These streets were paved with river pebbles, the central section (generally used by pedestrians) lined with slabs, known as lasagna, under which ran drains. At the beginning, low down on the corner, there is a reused roman paving stone, with a Roman game.

HOUSE OF ROMEO

Traditionally held to be where Romeo Montecchi (Montague) lived, it is certainly a house of the period in which Romeo would have lived, in the area in which he may have lived, and gives an idea of how he would have lived. It almost certainly belonged to the Nogarola allies of the ruling Scala family. A rich merchant's house of the 1200s, with warehouse at the ground-floor, at the second level the family's apartments, third for servants, and finally granary, kitchens and various. Later, while the inhabitations of the upper class became more sumptuous, it survived because well adapted to be used as a stable with Inn attached. Part of the building is still occupied by a typical Veronese "osteria" (pub), where you can still taste traditional dishes like "pasta e fasoi" (beans and pasta soup), "polenta e osei" (polenta - a kind of maize pudding - with birds), "polenta e bacalà" (polenta and stockfish), la "pastisada de caval" (horse meat), le "trippe" (interiors), ecc.

PIAZZA DELLE POSTE (The Post-office Square)

Once the a private garden of the Scala family (here Romeo and Juliet probably met), it became Verona's Botanical Garden, of which remain two Ginko Biloba trees, a Cedar of Lebanon, and a gigantic Elm. Here there is an impressive 20th century post-office in style by Fagiuoli, testament to the eclectic trends in architecture still present in this period. The **Teatro Nuovo** (New Theatre) had been build in the 1800s, attaching it to Juliet's House.

CASA DI GIULIETTA
(House of Juliet)

The house, for centuries identified as that of Juliet, is roughly half way down Via Cappello. A hat (cappello), on the inside of the entrance arch, may identify it as having belonged to the Capuleti (Capulet) family. It already existed in the XII century, and is the unification of several houses around an internal courtyard. The possibility of closing the courtyard, to be used as a stable, ensured its survival. In the courtyard there is a statue of Juliet. Traditions have grown up around it. Rubbing the breast, one will be fortunate in love. A Birthday has been decided upon, and people place flowers around the statue. Moreover, the love-lorn of the world address her letters, which are then responded to. The inside has been decorated in the style of a rich, 14th century merchant's house, and period ceramics collected for it.

Sources for the story - An obscure passage in Dante's Divine Comedy, which refers to the Montecchi grieving, may be the first literary mention of the tragedy. The story came to the notice of Shakespeare, by way of an account by

Below: House of Juliet.

Matteo
B a n d e l l o
priest, courtesan, and collector of scurrilous stories, who had it in turn from Luigi Da Porta (from Vicenza nearby Verona) who was simply reporting common knowledge.

The Story - Romeo and Juliet met one night at a masked ball and fell desperately in love, but she was a Capulet and he was a Montague, and the two families were enemies. The lovers met in secret for some time, she aided by her maid, he by a friar. One day, however, Romeo was walking through the streets of Verona together with his friend Mercutio, when he came across one of the Capulets, a cousin of Juliet, who insisted on fighting. Romeo tried to refuse, but, in that period, not accepting a challenge was a sign of cowardice, so his friend Mercutio accepted the duel, on Romeo's behalf, to save his honour, paying with his life. At this point Romeo, enraged, killed the Capulet and was condemned to exile. Desperate, he recounted everything to his beloved Juliet, and the two decided to get married immediately in secret. The friar, their friend, married them. That night Romeo entered the Capulets' courtyard, climbed up the balcony and spent the night with Juliet. In the morning, however, he had to leave for exile in Mantua. After a while, Juliet's parents decided she had to marry somebody else. She tried to refuse or postpone the marriage, but in that period it was the parents' decision and that was that. She went to the friar to ask for advice and he gave her a herbal infusion to make her seem dead for 48 hours. In the meantime he was to go to Romeo, who was to come back and rescue her, so that they could elope ... but the friar didn't reach Romeo. Having arrived at the gates of Mantua, he found them closed: there had been cases of plague in the Padana plain, and the people in Mantua were afraid of the illness, so nobody was allowed to enter to city. Romeo had heard his beloved Juliet was dead and so, desperate, he got on his horse, rode to Verona, went to the Capulets' graves ... there she really was, apparently dead ... He gave her a last kiss and killed himself. When Juliet awoke, she found Romeo dead beside her, and she too decided she didn't want to live without him: she took his knife and killed herself. She was fourteen and he was sixteen, and the story is a true story, at least in its main lines.

VIA CAPPELLO

Via Cappello, whose name derives from the Capulets, follows the route of one of the two principal Roman streets, the NS one.

Biblioteca civica - Here there's the civic library, whose new part was built by Luigi Nervi after WW2, during which an allied bombing had destroyed the previous Church of St. Sebastian.

*Above left: Graffiti left by lovers in the House of Juliet;
Above left: Juliet's balcony;
Right: Bronze statue of Juliet.*

PORTA LEONA
(Lion's Gate)

One of the Roman gates of the city, the original name is not known, the present was acquired after the discovery of the nearby sarcophagus with its two lions.

Built in the Republican period, it was originally double, of stone and brick, with two defence towers, more than 20m. high, of bricks, with a polygonal base of 16 sides, the foundations of which are still visible. Faced with marble under Emperor Claudius (1st century AD), the writing above the arches records the names of the Magistrates who oversaw the work. Today, only part of the internal façade in marble is visible, and behind it one can see the Republican brick gate. On the Imperial gate, only three of the six framed windows remain, as well as half of the exedra that surrounded a statue.

The whole was decorated with statues, as evidenced by the holes which helped to secure them in place. Paolo Diacono, in his "Historia Langobardorum", narrates that the statues were thrown upon enemies during a siege.

Above: Porta Leone (Lion gate), base of a defence tower;
Left: Lion gate.

CHIESA DI SAN FERMO MAGGIORE (Greater San Fermo)

Here where, in 304 AD, the soldier saints Fermo and Rustico were martyred, there arose at least four churches in their honour, plus a fifth where they were held to have been kept prisoner. Their names literally mean Firm and Rustic placing them in that tradition which, from the late 4th century, in its thirst for the relics of early martyrs, uncovered graves, on the authority of Bishops or of visions, and, for want of documentation, gave them names which indicate generalised traits. Discovered only in the eighth century, they were paid their weight in gold.

The remains of a 5th century basilica is visible under the lower church. Rebuilt in the 8th century after the discovery of the Saints, it was again rebuilt, because of subsidence in the 11th. At this point, in order not to disturb the relics, a second was built above ground, on the same plan, the columns in the upper being the continuation of those below. Hence, the presence was felt equally in both parts.

Today the lower maintains the earlier Benedictine scheme; however, when in the 13th century the complex was transferred to the Franciscans, the upper was transformed into a single nave, in keeping with the particular needs of this order (simplicity and room for preaching).

Façade: This is a successful example of collaboration between epochs. The lower part, with its subtle pilaster strips and portal, belongs largely to the Romanesque period.

The pseudo-gallery, its blind-windows originally frescoed with Franciscan Saints, acts as a transition between this lower and the later, higher Gothic elements. The long Gothic windows continue the motif. Finally, again in the upper, Gothic, part, the red and white stripes, from Verona's Romanesque lexicon, create a horizontal movement in opposition to the upwards tendency, forming a harmonious whole. The grave on the left belongs to Aventino Fracastoro (1368), medical doctor to Cangrande (who died young of a stomach ache), member of the family which in the XVI century gave rise to another illustrious doctor, the first to describe the course of Syphilis (in a poem).

On the left side of the church there are the entrances to the lower church and the lateral door of the upper. This last has above it a statue of Saint Anthony of Padua, and a fresco with a glorification of the Madonna.

Inside - Desiring a simple space adapted to preaching, the Franciscans adopted a single nave plan in which, strangely, one's attention is drawn to every particular rather than impetuously towards the main altar. Moreover, the ceiling becomes one of the dominant elements.

Shunning ostentation, the Franciscans have often opted for the simplicity of wooden beams. Here, in the tradition of the church of San Zeno, this becomes an elaborate keel vault, from the arches of which 416 saints gaze down into the church.

The 14th and early 15th century frescoes are particularly fascinating. On the right wall, representing the 14th century tradition of rich narrative rather than meditative images, are stories of Franciscans preaching the Gospel in India where they meet with martyrdom. However, the Emperor of Delhi (as he is known) condemns to death their persecutor, who is then executed along with his family. Some devils collect their souls, while other dog-like devils eat their bodies. Further up on the same side,

Above: Church of San Fermo Maggiore, inside;
Below: the façade.

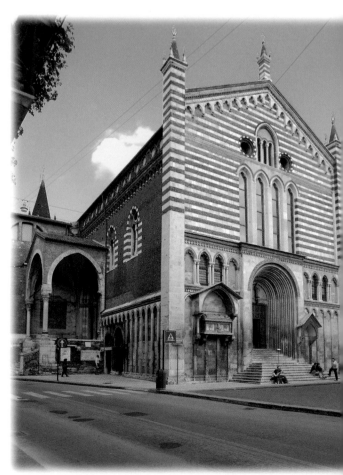

the pulpit (end of the 14th century) is surrounded by frescoes (Martino da Verona) which celebrate preaching by portraying, with an elaborately floral line, Evangelists and Doctors of The Church enthroned, and Prophets in Gothic frames.

At the main altar the artists seem not to have learned Giotto's lesson that architecture and landscape define real human presence.

Here there are representations of Christ the Redeemer, St John the Baptist and St Fermo, The Madonna and St Rustico, symbols of the Evangelists (the Animals and Angel), and Franciscan Saints. Some of these figures have an intense otherworldly presence, unusual, and in contrast with, dominant artistic trends. By another hand, framing the altar, there are an associate of the Scala family (Castelbarco) offering the rebuilt church, and opposite the Prior. Beneath, an Incoronation of the Virgin and an Adoration of The Magi in which buildings and landscape bear down on the figures.

At the very top there are two scrolls, the left smaller to emphasise that the arc is slightly asymmetrical (often the case, suggesting Christ's head which rolls to the side when he dies).

The relics of Fermo and Rustico have been at this altar since the 1700s, when successive floods made it necessary to move them from the lower church.

Over the lunette of the lateral door there is an expressive Crucifixion (Turone?), which, in the space it devotes to horses, armour, and the soldier Linus who puts Christ out of his misery, is a product of the courtly culture of the second half of the 14th century.

Down from this, the Florentine Nanni di Bartolo, representative of linear late Gothic sculpture (no longer in vogue in Renaissance Florence), has sculpted a Resurrection. Around it there are frescoes by one of the greatest exponents of Courtly Gothic painting: Pisanello. In addition to magnificent architecture, line and decoration, the Archangels Michael and Rafael appear, along with Gabriel in The Annunciation. Note that Mary has accepted the Angel's proposal and The Holy Spirit sends Christ, unusually a fully formed baby, down to her.

Amongst the later altars: on either side of the main altar there are paintings by Brusasorzi, fore-runner of Veronese, and Liberale da Verona, miniaturist (15th century). On the right there is the funeral chapel of the Alighieri, descendants of Dante. Near the lateral entrance opens the Chapel of the Madonna. Inside, glorifications of the role of Mary, including an unusual representation (Giarola) of a merciful Madonna who intercedes for the plague-stricken (1630) Verona with her vengeful, Jupiter-like Son and his distant, impassive Father.

Lower Church - Even after the removal of the relics it has a mystical atmosphere. It is at the level of the city in the Martyrdom's epoch, in the right side of the transept

there is the slab on which they are said to have been martyred. The church is lined with the tombs of those who wished to be buried close to their relics.

In origin, the columns continued in the upper basilica, giving the impression of being in a continuation of the crypt. The forest of columns, in four rows, alternate between square and cross forms creating lateral and diagonal rhythms.

Throughout there are frescoed six petaled flower-like motifs with circles: these are common to the area of the Po

Above: the sarcophagus of Antonio Pelacani;
Below: the gothic pulpit.

valley and may signify sun and universe. There are the remains of less obscure frescoes in many points, in a local version of pre-14th century trends.

Via Leoncino - The street, whose name clearly derives from the nearby gate, was formed by the line of houses built against the Roman city walls, remains of which can be seen in the internal courtyards. The street follows the course of the walls as far as the Arena. It was a prestigious road (also Maria Callas lived along this street with her Veronese husband), and some noticeable buildings can still be seen.

The Roman Domus in piazza Nogara - During works in the "Banca Popolare di Verona", remains of a Roman "domus" (house) came to light. It occupied some 400 square metres, with a central courtyard ("impluvium") on which the various rooms opened. It had been used from the 1st century b.C. to the 6th century A.D., as one sees from the superimposed levels of the floors. Fire damage links the destruction with the outbreak of a vast fire, probably the one which broke out in 590 A.D., described by Paolo Diacono in his "Historia Langobardorum". The southern part of the house, inhabited during the winter months, was heated by hot air obtained burning wood circulating underground, while the northern rooms where inhabited during the summer period, since they were cooler. After this discovery, the restoration plans for the bank changed in order to preserve the remains, which, thanks to a series of windows, are visible also from the outside. Inside, by means of a suspended walkway conceived of by Carlo Scarpa, it's possible to get close to the mosaics without ruining them.

PONTE NAVI (Ships Bridge)

So called because this area was the medieval port-zone. Damaged by the various floods and always rebuilt, the actual bridge was built after the II World War. During the Middle Ages the river was the major means of transport and communication. From the north rafts of wood came down with aboard raw materials and items from Germany: coal, fustian or moleskin, ironware (nails, hinges, iron bars worked by the local blacksmiths, etc.), and occasionally passengers as well. Some stopped in Verona and were discharged and dismantled, others continued on to Venice or the wares even farther afield (even to Egypt). In any case in Verona travel taxes were levelled on goods passing by. Upstream arrived goods from as far away as the Orient (silk, spices, precious vases, etc.) and especially salt, of which great quantities were necessary in the Middle Ages: to preserve food, for certain work processes (i.e. leather working) and for animal feed (cows, sheep, etc. need quite a lot of salt in their diets). These items arrived from Venice on wherries hauled by oxen or horses up a tow-path.

All these activities disappeared with the arrival of the railway road.

Also, during the many plagues, it was from this bridge that the ill were floated down towards the lazaretto situated in the Pestrino area, to the south of the city.

LA DOGANA (Customs)

Desired by the merchants of the 1700s in order to have a single, more practical point for disembarkation of merchandise, quarantining and disinfection. Built on a project by Alessandro Pompei, its classicism exalts the grandeur of Roman Verona and is therefore an expression of the desire for independence from Venice.

The Public Slaughter-house - For hygienical reasons and in order to centralize services due to population increase and the large number of Austrian soldiers, a new public slaughter-house was built at the beginning of the 1800s. Before this every butchery throughout the city slaughtered on its own account.

Above: San Fermo, the lower church, detail of the frescoes; Below: View of the Bell tower and apse.

The public slaughter-house was positioned at the end of the river's passage through the city, so as not to pollute the river, which at the time was still highly used. Inside there were also the "sborri", large rooms where goods where quarantined and purified with sulphur vapours. These were no longer necessary after the building of the new custom-house. The building's façade is decorated with ox's heads and the ceiling still preserves the tracks used for the moving of the carcasses. Today the area is occupied by artisans' shops, social areas and a restaurant, a fine example of the integration of industrial archaeology and modern uses.

VIA PALLONE
(Football Street)

The houses which had grown up here, leaning against the wall, were demolished to build the "Cittadella", the Visconti Milanese stronghold. In their place a defensive moat was dug. Filled in under the Venetian, the area became a playing ground for ball games.

MONUMENTAL CEMETERY

In the Roman period the law imposed burial far from inhabitations. In the Middle Ages the desire to be buried close to relics or in a place somehow holy, in addition to the fear of profanation, accentuated the tendency to bury in churches.In the 1700s, for reasons of hygiene, there was a movement to stop burial in and around churches, and in 1804 Napoleon emanated a decree to that effect. Verona, having entered a year later the French orbit, commissioned a new cemetery from Barbieri.

He chose the Doric style and may have had in mind a comparison between the Adige and the Greek Acheron (before the building of the Aleardi bridge the cemetery was reached by ferry paying a coin, like the shades reaching the Greek underworld). With the new rise of bourgeois and the consequent aggrandisement of the individual, sculptural funeral ornaments became a major form of artistic expression and here one finds some excellent examples.

CASERMA DI SANTA MARTA
(St. Marta Barracks)

Despite the name which should signify the field of Mars, the God of war has nothing to do with the area name. In fact it means marshy area, and was formed by a small river (Montorio), here deviated to build the Scala period walls.

During the Austrian period, the area, surrounded by walls but still free of buildings, became a barracks, because of its links with the railway station of Porta Vescovo (mainly used at the time as a military station). Here there were the barracks and everything needed to service the contingent (such as the bakery, that could produce bread and biscuits for hundreds of men and was used until after the WWII).

Below: Monumental cemetery.

TOMBA DI GIULIETTA
(Juliet's tomb)

Here, outside of the walls (because she died a suicide), tradition holds that the XIII century sarcophagus of Juliet is to be found. From the XVII century it has been object of pilgrimages, above all by English speakers, including Charles Dickens and Byron. Today civil marriages are held here.

The convent, San Francesco al Corso (13th cen.), has been used variously as an Orphanage, and as a military store-room. Today it is a museum of frescoes which outlived the buildings in which they were painted.

Inside. In the Roman epoch this area was rich in store-rooms. Down the stairs there are many amphorae, found in the course of restorations. Originally, they would have contained oil, wine, or "Garum" (fish sauce loved by the Romans). It's not known whether these amphorae were stored in a warehouse then covered by mud from the river, or were purposely used as a means of draining the terrain. In fact, for the Romans these were throw-away items, especially if they had contained oil or food which impregnated the recipient.

Often therefore they were thrown into the earth and were covered with gravel to drain swampy areas. These amphorae give us precious information on the commerce of the Roman city in as much as their form and the materials used in their making varied according to their contents and to the place of their making. Already in the Verona area wooden barrels and stone containers had been introduced and would eventually replace them. From the remains it is possible to deduce that "garum" fish sauce was arriving from Spain, wine from southern France and

southern Italy, and figs and dates from North-Africa.

Above, in the first two rooms there are XVI century frescoes by Brusasorzi and India, and afterwards of the 12th from the grotto of Sts.

Above: Roman amphora at Juliet's tomb;
Below: Juliet's tomb, the cloister.

Nazaro and Celso. There follows "The Music Room", XVI century frescoes by Farinati from the room of this function in Palazzo Guarienti. It is here that weddings are celebrated. At the top of the stairs which lead to the church there are Evangelists by Morone. In the cloister, a painting by Angelo Dall'Oca Bianca on one side, and bronze panels on the other side, describing the sad story of the two unfortunate lovers. Juliet's tomb is to be found in the crypt.

The "Montecchi" and "Capuleti" (Montegues and Capulets) in XIV century Verona.

They were two typical wealthy families, as is evident from their supposed houses, tall and build in bricks, when most edifices were still low and built of wood. Some have seen in the Capulets an alias for the Counts of San Bonifacio: Imperial nobles who ought to have been the legitimate governors of the city. Banned from Verona, they returned under the new name to keep in control of their proprieties. This theory explains the hatred between the two families, as rivalry between the old aristocracy and the nouveau riche. In this epoch the cult of Romantic love was been formed in poetical conventions, but marriage was still decided according to criteria of family advantage or economic advantage (in order not to disperse family assets or to advance socially – rich bourgeois who married poor nobles, or a political character), and personal preferences were not considered.

Above: The sarcophagus of Juliet; Below: Bronze panels recounting the lover's story.

CHIESA SS. TRINITA'
(Holy Trinity Church)

When, in the 11th century, parallels with Jerusalem were being sought, this hill was named The Mount of Olives, and a church built, perhaps by a crusader, certainly sponsored by Mathilda of Canossa, who supported the reconciliation of philo- imperial bishops with the Pope. The Vallombrosian monks of this church, in fact, were a mainstay of the reform of Gregory VII. Mathilda was decidedly in the Pope

confidence, so much so that it was her intercession which induced the Pope to remove the excommunication of Emperor Henry IV, not without having made him wait 3 days and nights, shoeless and dressed only in sack-cloth in mid-winter outside of the castle of Canossa (28th January 1077). The work of Mathilda, of which this church is part, confirmed her as one of the most important personages of the epoch, particularly remarkable if one considers that women rarely occupied pivotal positions at the time. After the earthquake of 1117 it was one of the few churches still in use and therefore its monks re-consecrated it in honour of The Trinity, Mary, and All Saints. In 1445 the monastery's function changed. Its produce became part of the Abbot's income, generally a noble Venetian residing elsewhere. While previously the abbots lived in the monastery and its profits (generally from rents) were reinvested in the monastery (to restore, enlarge or attract new monks who, in turn, brought money), now they went to Venice, creating a general impoverishment not only in the monastery, but in the whole city. The monks became so poor that in 1535 the monastery was abandoned by the monks and given to the "Convertite" (practically, a rest-homes for ex-prostitutes). At this point prostitution was tolerated and considered socially useful, given the diffusion of combined marriages in which it was often convenient to the partners not to have more contact than that strictly necessary for the production of offspring. Moreover, the practice preserved honest women from the attention of libertines, for it was a general idea that a woman alone (a widow without brothers to defend her, for example) could be molested. Nonetheless, prostitutes were considered deviant. Saint Augustine had written: "if the prostitutes are suppressed the passions will over-run the world and if the rank of honest women is conferred to them infamy and dishonour will corrupt the universe." It was normal, therefore, that, as soon as they had enough money, the prostitutes should try to redeem themselves. Just as it was normal that they should remain emarginated unless they found someone to marry. Hence the usefulness of these convents. In 1773 the Government of Venice suppressed the convent and confiscated its lands and goods. The church remained in function as a parish church. In 1945 it was damaged by

bombing.

Outside - The Church still has its narthex (a space reserved for penitents, who were not allowed to assist at functions).

Romanesque elements remain in the row of arches with double columns which allow light in (the larger windows are successive), in the prothyrum, in the red and white stripes and in the row of arches under the roof.

The belltower has robust supports, one of which rests on the head of a Medusa from the nearby Roman grave-yard.

Inside - In the atrium there is a 14th century sarcophagus reused when the Venetians began to bury their soldiers here, and 19th century gravestones from the period when it became necessary to bury outside the city. The church seems particularly long due to successive enlargements. Immediately inside, there is a raised loggia from which, masked by a grate, the ex-prostitutes could assist at functions.

The XVI century frescoes generally refer to their conversion to the path of righteousness: on the right, a conversion of St. Paul by Brusasorzi, by his father a St. Ursula with her 11,000 virgin martyrs (it seems they were in fact 11, the misunderstanding comes from their discovery in an ancient, crowded graveyard in Cologne), at the main altar, a Mystical Wedding of St. Catherine, again by

Brusasorzi. In the altar painting, by the same, there are Mary Magdalene and Saints who preferred death to the loss of their virtue.

Throughout, there are XIV century frescoes with miracles of Christ and moments from His life, and, in the altar, an Annunciation of the early 15th with stupendous Gothic edifices in the background.

Left: The church of the "Santissima Trinità" (Holy Trinity); Above: The Presbytery.

THE WALLS OF THE HILLS

From Porta San Giorgio (St. George's Gate, XVI cen., attributed to Falconetto), taking the Via dei Colli (Street of the Hills), one can see the various periods of the walls' construction: the part in white sandstone is Austrian, bastions and roundels are Venetian, while the part in sandstone, bricks and river stones are Scala period. At the top there are the Austrian fortifications: the Towers of Maximilian (Torricelle), and the fortresses which guarded Verona from being taken from behind. There are Forte Sofia (from the name of the Emperor Franz Josef's mother), Forte San Mattia, Castel San Felice, Forte delle Biondelle and Forte San Leonardo (Today the Sanctuary of the Madonna of Lourdes). Porta Vescovo (Bishop's Gate, XIV-XIX cen.), so called from the previous medieval gate, the taxes on good passing through having been the Bishop's rights, closes this stretch.

Above: "Porta Vescovo" (Bishop's gate);
Below: Sanctuary of the Madonna of Lourdes and particular of the statue.

SAN GIORGIO IN BRAIDA
(St. George at the Widening)

A church dedicated to George has existed here since the VIII century. The present however is fruit of a project begun in the XV. To Sanmichele we owe the Dome, the transept with the main altar, and the bell tower, which however remained unfinished because its height would have compromised the city's defences.

The *façade* is of the 1600s. Intended to form a whole with the adjacent Gate of St. George, those approaching perceived the two as one. The statues are of San Giorgio and San Lorenzo Giustiniani (one of the founders of the order who resided here).

The elegance of the facade contrasts with the edifice on the side, where there are still the wounds inflicted in 1805, during a French

bombardment of the Austrian section of the city.

The *inside* is of rare elegance. Goethe, in his account of Verona, defines St George "a church of good paintings". In effect, it is a gallery of 16th and early 17th century canvasses. There are paintings by: Montemezzano, Ottino, Domenico Robusti (son of Tintoretto), Brusasorzi, India, Caroto, Farinati, Bonvicino, Dai Libri, Recchia, and De Stefani.

The two holy-water containers, surmounted by bronze statues of Saint George and Saint John the Baptist are of the XVI century. On the right the second chapel has an "Assumption with Saints" by Ottino, and the forth a "Three Angels in Glory with the Madonna" by F. Brusasorzi. The altar to the right of the transept has a copy of "San Barnabus Curing the Ill" by Paolo Veronese. (The original is now in Rouen). The colossal "Saint Jeromy" and "Saint Gregory" instead

are by Bernardino India, author also of the monochrome inserts above the cornice showing "David", "The Virtues" and "Moses". In the presbytery preceded by an "Annunciation" (two canvases) by Giovan Francesco Caroto, there is to the right, "The Multiplication of the Loaves and Fishes" by Paolo Farinati; to the left a "Fall of the Madonna in the Desert" by F. Brusasorzi and students. At the centre is the "Martyrdom of Saint George" by Veronese, a masterpiece. On the opposite wall, the altar under the organ shows "Saint Cecilia between Holy Martyrs" by Bonvicini. On either side are soldier martyrs by B. India. In the next chapel (4th left) a "Madonna with Her Girdle" by Girolamo dai Libri, surmounted in the lunette by an "Eternal Father" by D. Brusasorzi.

The third chapel contains a polyptych by Caroto. The central section portraying "Christ Carring His Cross", disappeared in the 1600s and was replaced with a "Saint Joseph" by Recchia. To the side there is an entrance to an oratory where one finds a fresco known as "Christ of the Herbs", held to have been painted by a Venetian soldier on a defensive tower, using local plants to make his colour. It is held to be miraculous. In the successive chapel there is a "Martyrdom of saint Lawrence" by De Stefani and in the fourth and last "Saint Ursula and Companions" by Francesco Caroto. Above the entrance on the counter façade "The Baptism of Christ" by Tintoretto. Outside there is a cloister, all that remains of the antique monastery.

The section of river which follows on from San Giorgio is the part most changed by the building of the margins on the banks. As a matter of facts, after

the great flood of 1882 it was decided to built these. In this zone rows of houses were demolished (most of them already damaged by the flood) and eliminated the "Vo'", that is the alleys leading down onto the river. At the time this feat of engineering was regarded with great pride, having eliminated the risk of floods and lent the city a modern aspect. Today, however, many consider it a mistake, for the river has become totally extraneous to the life of the city. Moreover, little account had been taken of the elimination of centuries of history, tearing hundreds from their social context and initiating the building of quarters beyond the walls, destroying edifices of great artistic merit, and, above all, decreeing the end of all those activities which used the river (washerwomen, mills, river transport, factories, etc.). Activities however already in crisis with the advent of electricity and the railway.

Left: Façade of S. Giorgio in Braida.
Above: inside. Below: A foreshortening.

SANTO STEFANO
(The church of St. Stephen)

Founded in the 4th century, on the site of a Temple of Isis. In origin a Martyrium glorifying the Martyrs, it was dedicated to Stephen, first martyr, after the discovery of his remains, near Jerusalem, in the 5th century. Oddly, there are several examples of St. Stephen honoured on the site of this Oriental resurrection cult.

For some time, starting in 421AD, the Bishops of Verona were buried here and it may therefore have had Cathedral functions.

During the "Barbarian" domination, it was reworked several times. Under the Lombards, it was transformed, from a single nave to its present three, in order to construct the, now closed, Matroneum (gallery for women). Being a parish church it was presumably necessary to discourage promiscuity.

It also shows signs of having been oriented towards the West, according to

Arian usage. The Lombards were evangelised, before their invasion of Italy, by the followers of Arius (declared heretical by the Roman/Orthodox confessions). They certainly needed churches separate from those of the indigenous population. Perhaps this was one.

Façade - In the lower part there are the traces of inscriptions which record memorable events. The upper is typically Veronese Romanesque, from after the earthquake of 1117, with its red and white horizontal stripes. Two pilaster strips mark the position of the naves. The prothyrum and row of small arches are again Romanesque motifs.

The long and round windows were added in the 19th century. Original however, and unusual, are the little cross window with its two eyes. Also foreign to the local tradition is the octagonal central bell tower with its two-light windows.

Inside - Its function as a sanctuary of the Martyrs is the leitmotif which unites the periods of its construction, and attests to its importance throughout the ages. Entering, on the right there is the early 17th century chapel of The Innocents, celebrating the relics of 4 "Innocents" (the babies massacred by Herod), 40 Martyrs and 5 Bishop Saints of Verona. Incredible example of Baroque art with coloured marbles, golden stuccoes, cariatids, cherubs,

frescoes and paintings.

The authors include Ottino, l'Orbetto, Bassetti, del Moro. The subjects represented are stories associated with the relics, and with St. Stephen.

The area preceding the main altar of the church is particularly raised, emphasising the presence of the crypt, and there is a walkway around the apse which permitted one to walk around the relics.

The columns have capitals from various older buildings. Visible are fragments of XII and XIV century frescoes. In this area one finds a "Cathedra" (Bishops throne), perhaps of the VIII century. The crypt (X century), occupies the whole area beneath the transept and presbytery. The crossed vaults, decorated with Martyr's crowns and palms, rest on columns and capitals of the VIII century, with the exception of the four central, which are Roman, in Egyptian porphyry. Here too there is a raised walkway around the apse.

Given the importance of the cult of Relics it is not surprising to find works of art which today seem to clash with the period of the church. For example, the central vault with Christ, Evangelists, choirs of Angels, and instruments of the Passion, is of the

XVI century by Brusasorzi. In addition, from the same period, there are monochrome frescoes glorifying St. Stephen.

Page 100, on top: Inside of the church of Santo Stefano;

Left: The façade;
Above: The octagonal Bell tower.

S.GIOVANNI IN VALLE
(St. John in the Valley)

A cemetery church of the late Roman Empire, built on the site of a Temple of The Sun. It was used by the Arian Christian invaders, becoming St John of the Goths. In the VII century it returned to the Roman cult. In this epoch began the construction of the upper church, rebuilt after the earthquake of 1117.

Outside one admires the remains of its cloister, and the Romanesque bell-tower (with additions of the XVI century). Instead, of the 14th are the door, and hanging porch, with a Madonna and Saints, attributed to Stefano da Verona.

Inside, the whole was originally frescoed. The naves lead towards a crypt for relics, and, in consequence, a raised main altar, decorated in the Baroque period.

Amongst the changes of the Arian period can surely be included the little side apse to the North.

The crypt is divided in two. The ruder, heavier part is probably what remains of

the original church. Here there are two sarcophagi: that on the right contained relics of Sts. Simon and Judah, that on the left is simply the tomb of a third century AD couple. The pavement here is original.

L'ostello (The Youth Hostel) - The youth hostel is in the zone, in a villa of the 500s: Villa Francescati, with its

beautiful garden from which one has a fine panoramic view of the city.

Borgo Tascherio - In the Barbarian period this zone, for the ease of its defence, was inhabited by people of Germanic origin. Of different religion and culture, the Germans remained separated from the Roman inhabitants. Small in number, only the Germanic inhabitants could carry arms. Hence the name applied to them: "Arimanni", i.e. free men. It's for this reason that the feudal nobility was of German origin. The area's name, Borgo Tascherio, is due to the presence of the royal tax collectors, and comes from "tasche", the deep purses in which they collected

the taxes. In the Visconti period this zone was closed, using the pre-existing walls, and transformed into a military citadel.

Left: San Giovanni in Valle;
Above: The sarcophagus known as
"The arc of Sts. Simeone and
Giuda";
Below: detail of sarcophagus.

103

THE HILL OF SAN PIETRO (St. Peter)

Inhabited since prehistory, enclosed within walls in the period of the Roman Republic, in the Imperial Roman epoch it became a scenic backdrop to the city with the construction of a crowning temple. Dozens of houses and villas were expropriated to make way for this, including that of the poet Catullus. In the Christian period the temple was replaced by the church of St. Peter, from which the hill takes its name. Transformed in military stronghold during the Barbarian period, King Theodoric built here his palace. It was here that the tragedy of Rosamund unfolded, and here that Berengario King of Italy was killed.

Enclosed again in the Scala period walls, in the Milanese Visconti period

two castles were built here: San Felice and San Pietro, not immediately finished because of doubts about damaging St. Peter's church. Completed under the Venetian domination, these castles were destroyed when Napoleon ceded the area to Austria. In their stead, the Austrians built the actual building which functioned as a barracks.

This was served by a cable car, whose station can still be seen.

The Story of Rosamund.

- Alboin, king of the Longobards, having conquered Verona, made his residence the Palace of Theodoric on top of St. Peter's Hill, and it is here that the tragic story of Rosamund is set. Alboin conquered the Gepids, murdered their king, married the king's daughter Rosamund (usage transmitted Kingship through the female line) and made a drinking tankard of the king's skull. One evening, drunk at a banquet, he obliged Rosamund to sup from the mug. In vengeance, she had her lover kill Alboin. Soon however, maltreated by this new companion, she poisoned his drink. After a first sip, he realized that something was amiss, and obliged Rosamund to drink as well.

The comic stories of Bertoldo, Bertoldino and Caccasenno

are also set at the court of Alboin. Bertoldo, a simple farmer, always gets the better of the King. For instance: Bertoldo refused to bow to his King, so Alboin lowered the entrance to his throne-room. He then summoned Bertoldo. Not giving himself for bested, Bertoldo entered backwards, showing his hind-quarters to the King. Condemmed to be hanged for this outrage, Bertoldo asked, as his last wish, to choose the place of his hanging. The King magnaminously granted the request, and Bertoldo pointed to a strawberry plant. Bound by his word, Alboin accepted that he'd been outwitted.

View of the hill of San Pietro.

THE ROMAN THEATRE

With the transfer of Verona to the valley, the original Verona, the hill of San Pietro, was transformed into a scenographic back-drop. An enormous theatrical complex surmouted by a Temple, visible from the entire city, was built here. The theatre, constructed around 25BC, is one of the first Roman theatres to have been built in stone. In origin comprising a vast area between Ponte Pietra and a second bridge, Ponte Postumio, it also included an Odeon (a smaller covered theatre). With the collapse of Ponte Postumio part of the stage was demolished allowing traffic to pass in front along the banks. Earthquakes, floods, and laws inviting the people to dismantle the stones for new buildings, did the rest. In time, the area came to be covered with houses. A Church and Monastery still exist on the site. However, in the 1800s Andrea Monga bought the area, demolished some 30 edifices and started to dig.

One enters by way of a sixteenth century house built onto the stage walls. The theatre was built with stone quarried from the hill, probably then painted. The decoration and columns

were in marble. The stage, with its crowning decoration, in origin as high as the Cavea or seats, has largely been lost with the exception of some lateral elements.

Underneath the stage was a ditch used to create special effects, and beside a smaller indentation which held the curtains. In front, there was the semi-circular orchestra. The pavement, in this area, is original.

The Cavea, the semi-circle of white stone steps where spectators sat, was divided vertically into five sections by red marble steps (integrated with red-brick during restoration), and horizontally in three zones by corridors. Under the bottom steps there were drains.

The centre rests directly on the hill, while the sides were supported by embracing walls, in which ran access galleries.

The whole was crowned by a portico, with

a series of arches. On the inside of these are engraved the names of families which had financed construction.

Finally, there were a series of three scenographic terraces, the lowest where the 15th century monastery is today, and, at the summit of the hill, a temple where the Austrian barracks stands today.

THE ARCHEOLOGICAL MUSEUM

Above the Cavea, in the antique monastery, there is the Archaeological Museum. It contains pieces generally from Verona and

its territory. In the lower room are conserved fragments of cornices in marble, statue bases and a mosaic portraying Bacchus, which probably adorned a "triclinium" (dining room).

Roman mosaics - Originally a technique for waterproofing pavements, they were first to be found in courtyards and representation rooms, and later in the whole house, especially kitchens and toilets. They were also widely used in thermal baths, also on the walls, and in fountains. Originally made from pebbles, eventually small stones, sliced and fitted together, were used. In time, the technique improved and wooden boards were positioned on pressed levelled earth. Above these, stones as thick as a fist were laid and covered with smaller stones and then fine gravel. A level of cement was spread, and the decoration laid. Finally the floor was levelled and covered with marble dust sand and lime which united and protected the elements. From geometrical black and white designs, there was a movement, especially in wealthy houses and public buildings, to more colourful and elaborated patterns. Oftentimes in a room destined to contain furniture, the areas most likely to be covered were geometrically decorated, while the centre had a more elaborate decoration with scenes.

An opening in the pavement utilized as a well in past centuries consents a view of the gap – 20 metres deep and more than 100 metres long – which the Romans excavated to insulate the theatre from water damage. A staircase

View and detail of the Roman theatre;

On pages 108-109 view of the hill of San Pietro and Ponte Pietra.

leads to the monastery cloister, with inscriptions and funeral stones. On the left there is the entrance to the Chapel of Saint Jerome, protector of the Gesuati, with frescoes from the beginning of the XVI century. Here there are mosaics. To the right, instead, one enters the courtyard of the refectory. Fine frescoes adorned the walls, but only fragments of a "Last Supper" remain. A mosaic of the III century is inserted in the pavement.

There are altars, statue bases, statues such as the Cybele with her multitude of breasts. Interesting is the bust with elaborate breast-plate, collocated beside a series of heads. On the election of a new Emperor, old heads were often simply replaced. There are sarcophagi and funerary urns: burial and cremation co-existing in ancient Rome. Moreover, there are every-day objects such as glass containers for domestic and funerary uses. In the Roman period glass was a prized material, which generally came from Aquileia. The master glass makers with the Barbarian invasions moved onto the Venetian lagoon, where the tradition continues, mainly on the island of Murano. To the quartz sand was added a quantity of soda, obtained in the combustion of non-resinous plants and seaweeds, which made their glass particularly modellable. The mixture was fired a first time, smashed and refired with the addition of colour, then modelled with heat and by blowing. These glass objects are 2000 years old but could have been made yesterday by a master glass maker, with regards to design and technique. They were placed in tombs to hold aromatic oils, balsam, but above all the tears of the mourners.

Many bronzes can also be seen. They were generally made with the lost-wax process. Over an earthen model was spread a layer of wax, casing was placed over this, leaving opportune

Below: Archaeological Museum, mosaic;
Right: Statue of seated woman.

111

holes. This was then fired so that the wax melted, leaving a gap into which the bronze flowed. It is a very difficult technique, because one has to calculate the exact quantity of bronze and where to insert it avoiding air bubbles, gaps and fractures. The casing was then smashed, the bronze refinished and the earth inside extracted. This system of fusion was extremely expensive and didn't permit the making of more than one copy. For smaller items stamps were used, allowing them to be made in series. This option, however, would have proved too expensive and heavy in the larger objects.

One can also notice building decorations, fragments of bricks with their workshop stamp. On one of these there is the imprint of a child's foot. Children routinely worked in these factories.

From the windows, a wonderful view over the theatre and the city.

Below: mosaic;
Right: remains of the decoration of the Roman Theatre.

PONTE PIETRA
(Stone Bridge)

Known as "the stone bridge" because it remained a long the only one in stone. Of the 1st century BC, it is the oldest in Verona, predating by some years, in fact, the construction of the Roman city. Linking the two banks at the river's narrowest point, in origin it didn't follow the course of the Roman road.

The two arches closest to the theatre are the remains of the Roman structure, those towards the other bank were rebuilt at the end of the 1200s, by Alberto 1st of the Scala, along with the tower which defends it. The middle is Venetian of the 1500s. To better resist floods, holes were inserted: the circles Venetian, the arcs Roman. In this last section, a Roman River God also does

Left and below: view of Ponte Pietra and particular of its protective divinity.

his part.
Like the other bridges it was destroyed by the Germans at the end of WWII, then rebuilt, as it had been, with the original materials.

Panorama of the bridge and river.

SANTA MARIA IN ORGANO
(Saint Mary in Organon)

The name is said to derive from a nearby Roman construction known as the "organum", but, in all probability, comes from the German "morgen" (morning) being adjacent to the most oriental city Gate. In any case, an organ became the Stem of the monastery. The first mention of the church dates to 720, when the Longobard King, Liutprando, conceded it the right to tax goods passing over a nearby canal. In 1444 it passed to the Olivetan Monks, who gave it its present aspect.

Before the 1885 construction of the river margins, the church faced directly on a branch of the river, the "Canale dell'Acqua Morta" (Canal of Dead Water), filled in and become a street of the same name. A bridge connected it to an island in front (Today's Piazza Isolo). It was reminiscent therefore of the churches of Venice, with the façade reflected in the canal.

The **facade**, incomplete, was planned by Sanmichele. The bell-tower is also Renaissance, on a design by Brother Giovanni da Verona.

Inside, the body of the church consists of two distinct areas: the first, with three naves, and beyond, a raised presbytery and transept.

The central nave has a barrel vault and above the arches frescoes representing stories from the Old Testament, by Nicolò Giolfino on the right, while those to the left are of uncertain authorship. The organ above the entrance merits a special mention. The raised chapels, four on each side, have barrel vault and noble shields at the centre. Among the most important: on the right, the first with a "Mystic Wedding of St. Catherine" by Antonio

Balestra, and the fourth with a "St. Michael Archangel" by Paolo Farinati; on the left, the first with a "Madonna of the Rosary" by Antonio Balestra, and the third with a "Madonna in Throne with Christ-child and Saints" by Francesco Morone. In the transept frescoes traditionally attributed to Domenico Morone, on the vault a series of round paintings with Evangelists and Doctors of the Church. On the dome a crown of music-making Angels. To the right, the Chapel of St. Francesca Romana, the architecture by Francesco da Castello and frescoes by Cavazzola and Torbido. To the left, the Chapel of Bernardo Tolomei with a painting by Luca Giordano. In the Presbytery there

are two lateral canvas by Paolo Farinati (1566), representing episodes from the Massacre of the Innocents. Beneath, 16th century stalls in nut and the Easter candelabrum, all by Giovanni da Verona. Interesting is the statue in painted olive wood, of the XIII century, representing Christ on the ass, when He entered Jerusalem on Palm Sunday, which the Veronese carry in solemn procession on this occasion. At the centre, the main altar in Baroque style. The apsidal chapel on the right, dedicated to St. Helen, was frescoed by Nicolò Giolfino, that to the left, dedicated to St. Benedict, by D. Brusasorzi. The canvases are by Brentana. Beyond the 18th century

balustrade there are the choir stalls, with an elegant lectern in wood inlayed by Giovanni da Verona, made between 1493-1501 and rich in symbolic significance.

The **Sacristy** is one of the most beautiful in Italy, frescoed by Morone, with an Ascension, in the ceiling, and representations of Benedictine Popes. At the altar there is an Ecstasy of St. Francis, by A. Turchi, known as the

Left: Santa Maria in Organo;
Above: detail of the choir.

Orbetto. Once again, the inlays and carving of the back are by Giovanni da Verona, his last works. To the left are long wardrobes with seats decorated with oils by Agostino Brusasorzi.

Originally in the lower church, here conserved is an altar decoration by Giovanni di Rigino of the XIV century.

Underneath the Presbyterian part, there is the **original church of the VII century**, divided into three naves by columns of Roman origin.

Right: Santa Maria in Organo, lower church;
Below: the Sacristy.

GIARDINO GIUSTI
(Giusti Garden)

Planted in the XVI century by the Giusti family behind their Palace, utilizing the hill and its sand-stone, it became famous to such a degree that the family became "Giusti of The Garden". The lower part, more regular, is a typical Italian garden, decorated with statues and fountains and one of the first hedge labyrinths. However, led by a Cypress lined path, the eye is drawn to the higher "wilder" section, which rests on the hill, at the center of which there is a great Grottesque Manerist mask which spouted tongues of fire. Above this there is a "Belvedere" with a view over the city, and, to the side, grottos designed to provide echoes and to enable voices to be heard from other parts and odd perspective effects.

In these pages and the next: the Giusti garden.

SAN NAZZARO
(The Church of St. Nazaro)

In the fourth century a grotto was excavated to contain the relics of the martyrs Sts. Nazaro and Celso, brought from St. Ambrogio's Milan as part of the organisation and diffusion of the early Christian cult. The church was completely frescoed (the remains of these frescoes can be seen at the tomb of Romeo and Juliet). For its beauty it was cited in the first Guide of Verona, the poem the "Ritmo Pipiniano" (8th cen.). Repeatedly destroyed, the present church dates from the XV century.

After the treaty of Luneville, with the division of the city, it was proclaimed Cathedral of Veronetta, the Austrian section of the city. In 1810, with the Napoleonic closure, it was, in part, sold as a soap factory.

One enters by way of a peculiar portal sporting sculpted knotted drapes which have become proverbial: a girl without dowry was advised to take her wedding sheets from St Nazaro; if someone had little desire to work he could mop the sweat from his brow with the sheets of St Nazaro.

Architecturally the church is transitional between Gothic and Renaissance, rejecting somewhat the upwards development of the Gothic. It is enriched with side chapels containing paintings by some of the finest local artists of the 16th century, such as India, Farinati, Brusasorzi and Badile. In the transept, presbytery and abside there are frescoes by Paolo Farinati.

To honour the relics of Sts. Biagio and Giuliana, (brought home by Crusaders),

a chapel was begun, on the left, in 1488, which is one of the masterpieces of the Veneto Renaissance, with trompe-l'oile by Gian Maria Falconetto, who frescoed the whole alongside Francesco and Domenico Morone.

LA CHIESA DI SANTA TOSCANA (The Church of St. Toscana)

This was the area where St. Toscana lived in the XIII century, assisting the ill of the nearby hospital of Santo Sepolcro. She donated her possessions to the poors. In sign of humility, she wished to be buried along the public road. The citizens however, to avoid walking on top of her, diverted the road and over her body built the church of Saint Toscana.

Above: Church of San Nazaro, entrance of the "sagrato" (parvis); Left: the chapel of San Biagio.

MUSEO DI STORIA NATURALE (Museum of Natural Science)

Palazzo Pompei (Sanmichele, 1530). The building was donated to the city in the 1800s to house a museum which has become one of the most noted for the quality of its fossils unearthed in the area. In its rooms are explained the evolution of life on Earth. There are also interesting exhibits regarding the prehistoric inhabitants of the area.

Right: façade of the Museum.

SAN TOMASO (The church of St. Thomas)

Dedicated to St.Thomas of Canterbury, champion of the clergy's exemption from State taxation, who for his troubles was murdered in Canterbury Cathedral, probably by the henchmen of Henry II of England. Fifteen years later, in 1185 when a first church was dedicated to him, relics of the Saint had been given to the monks by a visiting Pope, part of the violent effort in this period to define the respective roles of Church and Civic powers. His cult was so diffuse and strong that Henry II himself was forced to do penance for the murder. Sanctuaries of his relics drew pilgrims for hundreds of years: Chaucer's pilgrims in The Canterbury Tales intend to pay their respects to him. In England itself the relics were swept away during the Protestant Reformation.

Ironically, in 1805, Napoleon made the monastery a barracks and the church a military hospital. Under the Austrians it became a military prison.

The actual church dates from the 15th century, and, in addition to the relics, contains the tomb of Sanmichele. Moreover, the Baroque organ was used by Mozart when he visited at 13. He also carved his initials on it.

Left: church of San Tommaso, the organ used by Mozart. Above: the rose window;

On pages 126, 127: night view of Ponte Pietra.

INDEX

© Edizioni Kina Italia/L.E.G.O. - Italy
Printed by: Kina Italia/L.E.G.O. - Italy
Distributed esclusively by: Souvenir Dimeno s.r.l. - Verona
Photos: Souvenir Dimeno s.r.l. - Verona
Particular thanks to:
Association of Guides "Juliet & Co."- Verona. Tel. 045-8103173